Minneapolis Underworld

Over a Century of Mill City
Racketeering and Collusion

Elizabeth Johanneck

Elizabeth Johanneck

All rights reserved.

Copyright © 2013

First Edition

ISBN-13: 978-1478236672

Front Cover: The alley in which investigative journalist Walter Liggett was killed by an anonymous gunman.

Back Cover: Article from the Midwest American, published by Walter Liggett, after investigative journalist Howard Guilford was murdered in his car by an anonymous gunman.

www.mplsunderworld.com
mplsunderworld@yahoo.com

Notice: The information in this book is true to the best of the author's knowledge. The author offers it without guarantee. The author disclaims all liability in connection with the use of this book. All rights are reserved. No part of this book may be reproduced or transmitted in any form without prior written permission from the author, with the exception of brief quotations embodied in articles and reviews.

DEDICATION

It is with much gratitude that I acknowledge Carolyn Shriver for her important contribution to *Minneapolis Underworld*.

This book is dedicated to my parents, Lenus and Marie Johanneck, and my siblings Philip, Steve, Kevin, Bob, Jeff, Anne, Peter and Danny. I dedicate this work to my friend Melanie Dunlap who has been a faithful friend and researcher, and to Big Carl Lithander who has been with me, and supported me, through the writing of three books.

But most of all, I dedicate this book to my children, Geoff and Kasey, and their loved ones, Adriane, Jojo, Trey, and Jayvyn. It is an honor to leave you with this legacy.

CONTENTS

	How I Got Into This Mess	7
1	The Criminal Element	12
2	Prohibition	44
3	A Soft Spot for Racketeering	55
4	Pornography	90
5	Smuggling Rings	104
6	Gambling	116
7	Unions and Organized Crime	127
8	Minneapolis Journalist Murders	137
9	Minneapolis Organized Crime	155
10	Birth of the Baldies	180

INTRODUCTION

How I Got Into This Mess

Meeting Mr. X.

Big Carl and I arrived at Barnes and Noble for my book signing about 20 minutes early, and the meal I had just eaten at a local Asian restaurant was trying to decide whether it should leave before the event started or stay put for a while. In spite of my tummy's uncertainty, I selected a double chocolate brownie from the Starbucks' display case and ordered a small cup of coffee, with room for cream, before settling into a fat, comfortable chair next to Carl. I was restless. I hoisted myself out of the chair and stepped into the room where the book signing would take place. With time to kill before my presentation, I needed to decide which chapter I should read to the crowd.

I use the term "crowd" loosely. When I strode to the podium, set before several dozen chairs, and only one chair was occupied, I knew this book signing was going to be sparsely attended. I would be reading to a small gathering. Oh, dear.

"Don't be heartbroken if no one shows up; these things aren't very well-attended." I looked at the kind man who was waiting for the reading to begin and who wanted to spare my feelings. "Are you the author?"

I admitted I was.

"I've already read your book and I loved it."

We chatted about some of the gangsters in my book, *Twin Cities Prohibition; Minnesota's Blind Pigs and Bootleggers*. "So you're an expert on organized crime?" he asked.

"Oh, no," I replied. "From what you've told me, it sounds like *you're* the expert on organized crime."

Big Carl wandered into the room where the reading was to take place and selected a chair across the aisle from the gentleman who was beginning to look a little bit like a mobster to me, and struck up a conversation. I suddenly noticed the man's slicked-back hair. And how had I missed the dark glasses?

The bookstore manager arrived then, introduced me to the meager "crowd" and I began reading about my visit to underworld figure Kid Cann's grave. Generally the topic generates a good deal of discussion, but tonight the small audience was reserved. I resumed reading, noticing the gentleman I had spoken with earlier peeking at his watch. He stood up then and rushed toward the front of the room.

"Here's a letter for you," he whispered, placed it on the podium, then hurried away.

What delicious intrigue. I couldn't wait to finish the reading and the task of signing books so I could open the sealed business envelope to reveal the mystery inside. I eventually got my chance.

> *Dear Ms. Johanneck,*
>
> *I read your book and was impressed with the way you approach history. You covered the economic and political background as well as a brief biographical background of each major character.*
>
> *I am written about in four books on organized crime in the Downtown Minneapolis Library:*
>
> *1.   Minneapolis Organized Crime 1900 – 2000*
> *2.   Deuce Casper and the Baldies*
> *3.   They Call me Kid Cann*
> *4.   Tommy (The Bomber) Ogdahl*
>
> *What's the point? Having a fifty year background (supposedly) in organized*

crime, as well as being a friend of Al Capone's niece, I am a walking encyclopedia of this history.

You should write a book on the history of Minneapolis organized crime. You already know about Doc Ames and Kid Cann, but not about organized crime from 1960 until 2010.

All the people I know who ran things and/or are still running things are sick or very old. Pretty soon we will all be dead and this history will be lost. The writings about me are somewhat true and somewhat inaccurate. This could be a great opportunity for you.

Sincerely,
Mr. X

Well, goodness, now what am I supposed to do?

In 2012 Minnesota earned a D+ from the State Integrity Investigation compiled by the Center of Public Integrity, Global Integrity and Public Radio International. The report concluded that:

> *"It appears Minnesota has not had a rich history of political corruption requiring additional reform legislation and therefore it has not kept pace with other states which have incorporated laws to combat corruption."*

I would venture to say that these folks have not done their homework.

Left to my own devices, I'm not sure I would have written a book about the history of organized crime in Minneapolis, though I had a close brush with doing so when I wrote *Twin Cities Prohibition; Minnesota's Blind Pigs and Bootleggers.*

I find that crime holds a certain element of romance when told through yellowed newspaper articles and sepia photographs and mug shots. But as corruption draws closer to the present, it loses some of that luster. The crimes occurring within my lifetime I tend to view with self-righteousness and disgust. Sometimes I wonder if I am simply more tolerant of the past because people dressed much better at the turn of the century, and wore good-looking hats.

When I first considered accepting this assignment, which meant I would be working with Mr. X, I told my family. That created a little stir. I recall my significant other, Big Carl, and my 94-year-old dad carrying on a spirited discussion while relaxing on a glider swing in the shade of a sunburst locust tree on my parents' farm. My dad was in favor of it, but Carl was not so sure. Back and forth they swung, facing one another with their voices rising.

"He's a member of organized crime," Carl argued. "What does that tell you?"

"It tells me," my old dad replied, leaning forward to make a point, "that he knows a lot about crime."

In the end I did what I wanted, which is what usually happens. It is important to note that Mr. X did not commission this book and that I consider it a labor of love. I am willing to poke around in the business of criminals from the past, but have no interest in the state of organized crime in Minneapolis today. I'm standing on the edge of foolhardiness, just writing this book. There's no sense jumping in.

This was a tough task. I tried to draw a timeline, gleaning information one tiny piece at a time from newspaper archives and court documents. I was eventually able to flesh out the individuals, and the eras, generally categorizing them into types of vices. So much more could be written. The underworld takes many shapes in Minneapolis, from the conventional organized crime families to complicit politicians and sanctioned business organizations. You'll find them all in Minneapolis' criminal past. St. Paul has nothing on us.

It is not a stretch to suggest that, at the founding of Minneapolis, the amount of space between some of our officials and the common criminal was too narrow to shine a light. From robber barons to politicians on the dole, Minneapolis saw it all.

The capitalists from back East who settled the city in the mid -1800s, and who now rest under the largest tombstones in town, came here to turn a profit, pure and simple. We know these men from the names on our street signs and our city parks and by the counties named after them. They had connections to men with deep pockets and they used them.

At the other end of the spectrum were the humble immigrants, hard-scrabble and street-wise, who found in Minneapolis an environment hostile to the poor. They were willing to do whatever it took to feed and clothe their families. They found that the jobs and potential wealth offered in the handbills back East turned out to be empty promises.

The mighty scorned the common criminal in public, but shook hands with him clandestinely behind closed doors when he required some unsavory business or needed muscle for hire. The two had much in common and could accomplish more by working together than by going it alone. Sound unlikely?

Welcome to Minneapolis' underworld.

CHAPTER 1
THE CRIMINAL ELEMENT

A Letter from Mr. X

I wrote a brief letter to Mr. X and sent it to the return address on the envelope he had given me. I hadn't decided yet whether I would go ahead with this project of writing the history of organized crime in Minneapolis. On the one hand, it feels a little bit dangerous. After all, I don't want to get whacked by an angry hit man. On the flip side, a part of me feels like I've been working toward this all of my life. I need to find out more about this guy, this Mr. X.

> Dear Elizabeth,
> Thank you for your quick response. I would love to spend an hour (or probably less) discussing this book idea with you.
> I can meet you in the first week of September in your own neighborhood. We could just meet for coffee and a chocolate fudge brownie (I noticed you like brownies).
> If you can get your publisher interested in a book of Minneapolis organized crime, you will monopolize the market. In a few days I am going to mail you a very "yellow journalistic" manuscript (book) called *Minneapolis Organized Crime 1900 – 2000* that you can keep. This book is more contemporary covering current mob bosses and some activities.

Some of the book is inaccurate. My name is inaccurate and I am certainly not dead. This book is in the library, and I think you and your publisher can do a better job and compete with it, plus get it into Barnes and Noble.

I just want an accurate chapter on my impact.

Mr. X

P.S. I am a perfect gentleman, but considering you're a very attractive lady, feel free to bring your lover to our meeting.

Oh, who do I think I'm kidding? I know Big Carl isn't crazy about the idea of me spending time with an organized crime figure, but my curiosity has gotten the best of me. I often wondered, after writing *Twin Cities Prohibition,* if organized crime had really been eradicated in the Twin Cities or if it was like those spots of mold on my basement wall that disappeared when I scrubbed them with bleach and white-washed them, but reappeared again under just the right conditions.

Fine, I'll write the darned book. I mean, I'm sure any crime figure showing up in the manuscript will have already paid his debt to society. And let's face it, it *is* in my nature to talk about things that are probably better left alone. I should really know better.

ON THOSE WHO SETTLED MINNESOTA

The majority of the citizens are a class of speculators who have come here for the purpose of making money, and every means are resorted to, to induce persons in the East to come here . . . they do not intend to leave until they have their wants supplied, for this is a very good place for a man who has capital to make money; and there is but very few persons here who expect to make this their permanent home.

G.W.P
The Evening Post, May 5, 1857

South Minneapolis Born Out of a Swindle

Franklin Steele

"Many commit the same crimes with a very different result. One bears a cross for his crime; another a crown."

Satires (XIII, 103)

One of the earliest and most well-documented crimes recorded in the Minnesota Territory is a swindle committed by high profile individuals who somehow managed to achieve and maintain their standing as heroes in local history books. In 1857, the United States government was fleeced out of thousands of acres of Fort Snelling property, along the Minnesota River valley in a conspiracy orchestrated by United States

Secretary of War John B. Floyd and local businessman Franklin Steele. Steele was a brother-in-law to Henry Hastings Sibley who served as the first Governor of Minnesota. He was also an acquaintance of President James Buchanan who presided over the country when Steele's crooked purchase was made.

History books call the mysterious sale "a clandestine event" or "a moonlight caper." But the truth is that it was much more than that. It was an underworld arrangement between government officials and speculators. Floyd was eventually accused of being corrupt and ineffective as Secretary of War. He was found guilty of engaging in shady dealings involving padded government contracts later used as collateral bonds from an Indian trust at the Department of the Interior. The "moonlight caper" was written about in newspapers across our young nation and was officially reviewed by a commission headed by the Congressman from Indiana, John U. Pettit of the Select Committee of the 36th Congress. Under the authority of the resolution of the House of Representatives, Pettit issued a 400-page report (Report No. 351) about this crime. Of its efforts the committee reported that:

> "The committee had steadily been embarrassed from a difficulty in obtaining prompt answers from the War Department."

The report included a letter from the Hon. Henry M. Rice, delegate of the of the Minnesota Territory, one year earlier, on April 24, 1856. In his letter he stated that he received a proposal from Franklin Steele for the purchase of the Fort Snelling reservation and overflow lands to the tune of about five thousand acres, at $15 per acre for a total sum of $75,000. When the proposal was forwarded to Quartermaster General Thomas S. Jesup, Jesup wrote to then Secretary of War Jefferson Davis, and advised him that he felt a reduction in the size of the fort was possible.

> "The site is no longer of any value as a position for defense. Its only value now is a depot of supplies for frontier posts in advance of it. If the lands be sold, the fort, wharf, and the ground between the fort and water, with about one hundred and fifty acres, should be retained for public use, not temporarily, but in fee. I have been advised today that a higher bid may be expected."

Davis responded to Jesup:

> "In reply, I have to say that the reservation is still needed for military purposes, and Mr. Steele's offer cannot, therefore, be entertained."

In the following year of 1857, former Virginia Governor John B. Floyd was appointed Secretary of War by President James Buchanan. He began a career of corruption and deceit. Floyd sent artist and United State Army Major Seth Eastman to the Minnesota Territory to survey Fort Snelling property in preparation for the sale of the fort.

Dr. Archibald Graham of Lexington, Virginia, representing investors operating under the auspices of a New York company, heard from Secretary of War Floyd about several old forts for sale in Minnesota Territory. Graham asked Floyd if his department could help pay expenses for a trip to Minnesota. The New York investors included Graham and two New York Senators, John C. Mather and Richard Schell. Apparently having former social ties with Franklin Steele, who had been the army sutler (civilian merchant) at the post, the group induced Steele to join them as a co-purchaser of Fort Snelling.

William King Heiskell was appointed commissioner and assigned to make the sale of the fort at the very moment Graham was planning his trip to Minnesota. The two traveled as companions, staying in the same St. Paul hotel. Graham and Mather were both aware of Heiskell's status. Mather also traveled to Minnesota, conferring with Steele at the fort. The Secretary of War had also authorized Mather to go upstream and examine the Fort Ripley property for possible purchase.

Major Eastman and Heiskell both reported to the Secretary of War that, in their opinions, the value of the fort for military use had passed and the fort ought to be sold. Upon Mather's return to Fort Snelling, a sale was made, nominally, to Steele. Eastman and Heiskell, who oversaw the sale, later claimed they were completely unaware that Steele had partners. They defended themselves, explaining they had every intention of preventing combinations of investors from purchasing the land in order to prevent government loss.

The Investigative report contended that the sale was conducted with so much privacy that, outside of the Department of War and those directly involved in its purchase, no one had any inkling the fort was to be sold. Only the commissioners overseeing the sale, the buyers and Augustus Schell, lawyer, railroad magnate and Democrat politician from New York who loaned money to the investors, were aware.

Eastman told the Select Committee preparing its report that the Secretary of War planned to send an agent to sell the land. Eastman was not an agent, nor had he expected to become one. But he was soon granted agent status.

Graham declined the offer to be acting agent for the sale of the property, stating that he would instead prefer to be a purchaser. He had the great fortune of teaming up with Mather, Schell and Steele. Only one-third of the $90,000 sale price was initially paid to the U.S. Treasury in New York, with one-third of that sum provided by Steele and the remainder paid by Mather and Schell on July 2, 1857. No additional payments had yet been made, nor title conveyed, when suddenly, on July 31, 1857, the Department of War sent a dispatch to the officer in command of the fort. The officer was directed to surrender the land to Steele and to maintain the fort for military purposes under Steele's ownership, "until further orders."

It was a conspiracy in the making. Before Governor Floyd was appointed Secretary of War, he had been in a political race with Commissioner Heiskell and made his acquaintance. Floyd won a place in the legislature and Heiskell claimed he had remarked, jocularly:

> "Now old fellow, we have had a rather hard fight of it together against the know-nothings here, and when you get into office you must not forget me. I want you to give me a place. I want one that will pay not less than $4,000 - $5,000 a year. I don't want anything else."

To which Floyd responded:

> "If I can do anything for you, you shall have it."

In April Heiskell received a letter from Floyd about an assignment which would pay very well. He wanted him to travel to Minnesota because there was a reservation he wanted to sell. Floyd told Heiskell he wanted him to make the best sale ever in the United States. Floyd wrote:

> "You've got a parcel of sharpers to deal with, and you have got to keep your eyes open. I want you to execute the commission to the best of your judgment. You understand speculation; you understand mankind."

The report determined that the Secretary of War acted in secrecy and defiantly ignored the opinions of his peers in regard to the value of Fort Snelling as a military installation. According to the report, the fort was silently, and without suspicion, divested from the government "under its very feet." It was also determined that the price struck by Steele's group and the Secretary of War was far below its intrinsic value, had it been brought to market under more cautious and prudent manner. Concern was raised about the danger of valuable government land being purchased for less than its market value by unprincipled and lawless speculators who would use intimidation and threats of violence to prevent settlers from making offers on smaller parcels.

The report lamented the "pernicious and perilous" system of making public preferments the spoils of the successful side of politics. Never mind that the Secretary of War rewrote the law of the land with which to facilitate the sale of the property. Whereas the law stipulated property be conveyed to the purchaser when it was paid in full, Governor Floyd's representatives wrote the contract to convey the land upon the first payment. Where the law stated a military reservation could be sold only upon becoming useless, Floyd wrote into the contract stipulated possession "as soon as the Secretary of War could dispense with it for military reasons," as if this determination was the sole responsibility of Floyd.

Other local capitalists interested in purchasing the property were angry. Speculator Colonel Cyrus Aldrich of Minneapolis assured the investigating committee that there would have been no threat of combinations of investors had the land been made available to local investors. People in the vicinity were men of means, many of whom wanted parcels of the land for themselves, he said.

Commissioner Heiksell was questioned about the payment of the remaining $60,000 and admitted that no interest was being charged on the amount due because he "did not think of it." Now the government had become the tenant of a large portion of the land. Steele acknowledged he was in a position to now collect rent for the troops and two hundred horses, mules and oxen stationed there. Heiskell told the committee investigating the sale that he kept the price per acre low because, although he saw ploughs turning over beautiful black soil, he saw at the bottom of the burrow white sand. He would not give $2 an acre for the land, predicting in a couple of years the soil would be blown into sand banks.

The New York Times carried editorials about the event. One article published on September 25, 1857:

> Never was a profligate job covered up with a veil so flimsy, or excused by apologies so feeble. The next Congress will have something to do besides exposing malfeasances of its members. Meanwhile, it would be interesting to know how far Mr. Buchanan and his Cabinet are disposed to assume this operation of Secretary Floyd.

Another article in *The New York Times* was published April 14, 1858 with the title, *The New-Bedford, Fort Schuyler, and Fort Snelling Land Sales – Evidences of a Grand Plunder Combination of New-York Politicians*. That story shed a little more light on the affair, asking the question, "How could property judged to be worth no more than $200 per acre at Fort Schuyler near New Bedford suddenly leap to a value of $1,300 per acre?" The answer was simple. It was purchased from Mr. Bixby (the article does not mention Bixby's first name) of New York with a contract from the Secretary of War. Bixby, it turned out, headed a firm in which John C. Mather was a silent partner, along with Schell. The two transactions appear to have been orchestrated by a clique of seven men, all prominent politicians in the East.

Steele's land became part of south Minneapolis and he resided there as one of the wealthiest men in the city.

A Near International Incident

Lord Gordon Gordon

In the summer of 1871, a career racketeer of Scottish descent arrived in Minneapolis and registered as a guest at a local hotel. He signed his name G. Gordon and promptly deposited $20,000 worth of English pounds into a vault at the National Exchange Bank of Minneapolis. Within days, Gordon received a letter at his hotel addressed to *Lord* Gordon. The information filtered through the Minneapolis grapevine in a flash, causing a stir. The city was relatively small back then, with a population of about 20,000, so by contrast the news was substantial

A man of such obvious means soon found himself in a whirl of social activity as wealthy Minneapolis businessmen weighed his value as an investor and wives planned picnics and parties to show him off. To their delight, he spent money lavishly and talked about his family estates in England and Scotland. He shared his plans to purchase land for Scottish settlements. That caught the attention of Colonel J. Loomis, Land Commissioner for the Northern Pacific Railway. Loomis planned for a party of businessmen to travel along the rail line, which was making its way west. Guests on the trip were Gordon, Loomis' secretary and attorney, and surveyors George B. Wright and Nathan Butler.
The *Fergus Falls Daily Journal* carried descriptions of the event:

> "...a caravan of forty horses, twelve men to pitch tents, a French cook and a number of colored waiters wearing white linen aprons and white silk gloves."

Gordon was treated like royalty and was given two tents, a valet and secretary for his use. One wagon carried guns and tackle for fishing and deer hunting. They carried with them fourteen changes of clothing. Meals were served on china and silver. A surveyor was employed to gallop along and mark 50,000 acres of land as "sold" upon being selected by Gordon for his settlements. In the end, Loomis spent $15,000 - $45,000 on the two-month trip, declaring it an investment that would give a huge return with Gordon's promised $5,000,000 investment.

Gordon led the leaders of the city of Fergus Falls to believe he would send one hundred families, poor tenants of his from Scotland properties, to Pelican Lake in Otter Tail County in the spring of 1872. There they would settle in a new community to be named "Loomis."

Upon his return, Surveyor Butler was shown about twenty pieces of solid silver by Gordon, some of which, he was advised, were gifts from officials of the Northern Pacific Railroad.

The *New York Herald* newspaper reported in April, 1872, that the illustrious Gordon had remarked to an individual interested in the new community:

> "Aw my deaw fellah, as a fwend, I will let you have one cworner of a

stweet."

Just after the New Year, Gordon left Minneapolis for New York with letters of introduction from his new friends in Minneapolis. In the meantime, Loomis was preparing the sale of the land chosen by Gordon for his fictional settlers. Once in New York, this master racketeer met his nemesis and fellow swindler, Jay Gould, the king of the United States robber barons. Gould was known in the press as the most hated man in the country, a reckless speculator and heartless strikebreaker. He and his fellow robber baron, James Fisk, manipulated Wall Street with their wealth in 1869, causing an economic crash on September 24 of that year which became known as Black Friday. He was a master of bribery and stock manipulation and had no concern for the American people whose lives he destroyed.

Gordon lived quietly in New York for some time, using Loomis' letter of introduction to meet New York's elite, including Horace Greeley, newspaper editor and founder of the Liberal Republican Party. Greeley was a reformer, politician and an opponent of slavery. He was delighted with Gordon's fabricated plan for a settlement in Minnesota and tried to interest Gordon in some land in Virginia.

While in the city, Gordon stayed in room 110 at the Metropolitan Hotel of New York, paying over $150 a week for lodging with food and drink extra. New York was experiencing a post-Civil War speculative boom and corruption was at an all-time high. Gordon soon became friends with William Beldon, whose wife Gordon had met on a train to New York. Mrs. Beldon was also the first wife of financier James Fisk. In no time at all, Gordon was hob-knobbing with Gould, Fisk and Daniel Drew who were in competition with Beldon for control of the Erie Railroad, an organization whose stock was manipulated so often it became known as the "Scarlet Woman of Wall Street."

Gordon saw the opportunity to make a killing off the fortunes of these men and told Greeley that he owned sixty-thousand shares of Erie stock and had control of much more. He would be a useful man to know when the battle for control of the railroad began.

Greeley was delighted, because he saw a need for reform of the Scarlet Woman. Greeley carried the message of Gordon's Erie ties to Gould and the two made arrangements to meet. Gordon enchanted Gould with his lies about the land he had recently purchased in Minnesota and his ties to the royal family. He told Gould that he represented the English who controlled the Erie Railroad and that it was his desire to name three English directors to the board of the Erie Railroad. The other directors could be named by Gould, but Horace Greeley was to be one of them. Gould swallowed the deception hook, line and sinker. A business arrangement was agreed upon with Gould turning stocks and cash as security over to Gordon for his help gaining control of the railroad. The illusion was complete.

Gould basked in his victory for several weeks until he heard that Gordon was selling his stock. Gould took a look at the situation and devised a plan. He rented the room next to Gordon in his hotel and had a small crowd join him there, including the police chief and police justice. A representative presented his card to Gordon asking for an interview, which was granted. He expressed to Gordon Gould's desire to have his financial securities returned to him or Gordon would face arrest. Gordon returned all of the securities and cash, except for the six hundred shares of Erie stock which he had already sold, leaving Gould with even less control.

Gould filed a suit against Gordon and the court set his bail at $37,000, which he met with the help of bail-bondsman A. F. Roberts. He went to court to answer Gould's complaints, then quietly slipped across the border into Montreal, Canada.

Gould's attorney crossed the border to arrest Gordon, but found he had already made his way to Winnipeg, just north of Minnesota. Gordon registered as a guest at the Munro House initially, then boarded with Mrs. Abigail Corbett in Headingly for a time, where he was accepted as a member of the community.

In the summer of 1873, Minnesotans George N. Merriam, who would become the Governor of Minnesota, and the Honorable Loren Fletcher of Minneapolis were in Winnipeg selling lumber and fortuitously saw and recognized Gordon. They knew that some of their friends back in Minneapolis, taken for fools by Gordon, were looking for him. Merriam immediately contacted Minneapolis Mayor George A. Brackett who in turn alerted bail bondsman A. F. Roberts of Gordon's whereabouts and got a warrant for his arrest. According to the July 12, 1873, *Minnesota – Herald*, Brackett was advised by the firm of Lochren & McNair of

Minneapolis that a warrant could be issued in the United States for Gordon's arrest on the grounds that "wherever common law prevailed, such a document was effective regardless of national boundaries." The legal advice was not based on the Webster-Ashburton Treaty in regards to extradition and was, therefore, questionable. Upon receiving this

James J. Hill, Minnesota railroad baron (closest to camera)
Photo courtesy of the Hennepin County Library.

information, a plan for Gordon's arrest was developed.

Brackett sent Minneapolis police officers Michael Hoy and Owen Keegan by train to Breckenridge on July 26. From there the men drove a stagecoach to Fort Garry at the confluence of the Red and Assiniboine Rivers in what is now downtown Winnipeg. The two met with the Hon. Loren Fletcher, a member and later speaker in the Minnesota House of Representatives, and with former Minnesota resident and St. Anthony business owner L.R. Bentley at Portage Avenue and Main Street. There they completed the details of Gordon's arrest. The pair tried to be as secretive as possible, harboring some doubt as to the validity of their warrant. They also were concerned about how the community would react to Gordon's arrest.

The men located Gordon in Silver Heights at the residence of the Hon. James McKay, Governor of the Hudson Bay Company. Silver Heights centered social life on the banks of the Red River. Gordon had ingratiated himself with the upper crust in Winnipeg and was often a guest at gubernatorial dinners and on buffalo hunts. Previously, Jay Gould had tried to entice the young man back across the U.S. border with invitations to social events. But Gordon was not to be fooled.

The men seized Gordon, bound his arms and legs, and then threw him into the back of their wagon. Gordon's servant alerted the community of Winnipeg of the abduction and an armed rescue party managed to stop the kidnapping. Now it was the Minnesotans turn to be arrested. Officers Hoy and Keegan were detained and returned to Winnipeg on board the S.S. Dakota. In addition, the Hon. Loren Fletcher and George N. Merriam were arrested as accomplices and placed in the jail at Fort Garry. Fletcher sent a telegraphed message to Mayor Brackett in Minneapolis advising:

"I'm in a hell of a fix. Come at once."

Upon their arrest, $37,000 in lumber contract funds were taken from Fletcher and Merriam and placed in the hands of Attorney General Clarke for safe keeping. United States counselors were initially prevented from seeing the men and they would not forget this injustice.

A potential international incident was in the making when Brackett set off to Winnipeg with legal representation. He reached his destination on July 8 to rescue his officers and the hearing took a fortnight to conclude.

Tensions escalated between the United States and British Canada. Merriam was offered bail on July 26, but the other men involved in the kidnapping were not. Newspapers were preparing citizens for the possibility of war. Senator Alexander Ramsey and Minnesota Governor Horace Austin headed to Washington D.C. to visit the Assistant Secretary of State. But little help was offered, and Ramsey returned to Minnesota. Mayor Brackett took a trip East where he and Austin met with President Ulysses Grant in New Jersey. Grant asked for a written statement of the affair.

Washington began pressuring England, which responded with enquiries as to whether the prisoners could not be released on their own bond. They also questioned the location of the arrest—whether it actually occurred in British territory or on the American side. Federal interference was being considered while waiting for the men to be released. In the end, a special court was convened on September 16 and the prisoners were sentenced to twenty-four hours in jail.

A year later, the *Alexandria Gazette* reported that while the disliked Canadian Attorney General H. J. Clarke of Manitoba was leaving St. Paul to catch a train East, he was:

> . . . set upon by a crowd of ruffians from Minneapolis headed by Mike Hoy, Chief of Police of that city, who beat and kicked Clarke savagely, and but for interference of one or two other citizens, would doubtless have been killed.

Gordon did not suffer the same brutal fate as Clarke. However, although he escaped his captors, Gordon was not off the hook. He continued to dodge legal bullets from Gould and others. Then, one frigid night when a great blizzard raged, Canadian police arrived at Gordon's property with warrants for his arrest. He reportedly said to the police:

> "I can see it all. Jay Gould with this money has won. Away from Winnipeg, we shall be in St. Paul in a week with his money and influence at work it means conviction. I see what it all means, but needs must when the devil drives. A cold night, isn't it? I must wrap up. To St. Paul. I shall take a shorter road . . ."

He slipped into his bedroom and shot himself in the head. According to the Manitoba Historical Society, in the end, a Canadian, Dr. Chambers (first name not recorded), established the discovery of Gordon's father and sister:

> "They were of cultured, gentlemanly and ladylike manner and appearance, of an exceptionally good appearance, linguists of ability in the languages of Europe, travelled and well-spoken. However, they were leaders in a group that operated from the Isle of Jersey in the business of international smuggling."

First Godfather of Minneapolis

Albert Alonzo (Doc) Ames

"Every society gets the kind of criminal it deserves. What is also true is that every community gets the kind of law enforcement it insists on."
President John F. Kennedy

The first well-documented "Godfather of Crime" in Minneapolis was politician Albert Alonzo (Doc) Ames. Born in Garden Prairie, Illinois in 1842, Ames migrated as a child to Fort Snelling at the junction of the Minnesota and Mississippi Rivers in the southeastern Minnesota Territory in 1852. As a youth he delivered newspapers for the *Northwestern Democrat*, located at the southeast corner of Third Street and Fifth Avenue South in Minneapolis. He earned a medical degree from Rush Medical College in Chicago, returning to Minneapolis at age 22 to practice medicine with his father. He served as a medic in The U.S.-Dakota Conflict of 1862 during the time Governor Alexander Ramsey's administration was clearing the land of the indigenous population in order to free it up for sale to speculators.

During that time, around 1862, Ramsey had cryptically declared to the Minnesota State Legislature:

Governor Alexander Ramsey
Photo courtesy of the Hennepin County Library.

"The Sioux Indians of Minnesota must be exterminated or driven forever beyond the borders of the state."

He then offered the public a $25 bounty per scalp for every surviving Native American man, woman and child in the state.

Native Americans confined to the Lower Sioux Reservation. Photo courtesy of Gary Revier.

Ames was handsome, well-liked and vain. He was elected mayor of Minneapolis for the first time in 1876 and served in a variety of political positions after that, sometimes as a Democrat and sometimes as a Republican. Prior to that, Ames had moved to California where he was managing editor of the *Alta California* from 1868, through 1874. He returned to Minneapolis due to his father's failing health, taking over the family medical practice. He was kind to the poor, often waiving his fees for the destitute, and had the support of labor and the working class in Minneapolis.

It was at the outset of his fourth term as mayor in 1901 that Ames put into place a system of graft and corruption that won him a sordid place in Minneapolis history. His actions were carefully documented by Lincoln Steffens and published in *McClure's* magazine in 1904.

Steffens' article, titled "The Shame of Minneapolis," caught the attention of young Walter Liggett, luring him into the business of investigative journalism—a decision which would eventually lead to his grisly demise in an alley in Minneapolis three decades later.

In his final term as mayor, Ames was elected as a Republican reformer, though an opinion piece in the *St. Paul Globe* on April 16, 1901, suggested things weren't what they seemed. Ames' friends lauded the work of his administration and its new police chief by pointing to the fact that more stolen property had been recovered during his administration than any other. Ironically, it was his band of specially selected police officers who turned out to be the very thieves responsible for the thefts in the first place.

> The truth of the charge against Mayor Ames, that he was engaged in building up a political machine, has been, for all practical purposes, admitted. His goal in this regard was clear from the outset. His discharge of fifty percent of the police force, including men of years of experience and tried fidelity and capacity, was concededly the result of his purpose in this direction. He never thought it worth his while to deny the charge. To all the imputations cast on him and his administration, Ames unfailingly turned to his record of police recovery of stolen property—a record which might be read differently by different persons.

The opinion piece goes on to describe Ames' efforts to create a powerful one-party machine, putting Democratic police officers on the "charity of a cold world in the midst of winter" and calling it reform.

In order to understand the type of men Ames sought to take over the city of Minneapolis, one need only pay attention to a newspaper article in the *Kalamazoo Gazette* published on November 9, 1901. The newspaper reported that upon Cole Younger's release from Stillwater State Prison, after serving twenty-five years for an attempted bank robbery in Northfield, Minnesota, Ames offered Younger the position of captain on the Minneapolis police force. Younger, a former member of the James Gang, was on parole and working at a grocery store in St. Paul. He advised Mayor Ames that he did not wish to do anything that would not be just or right, nor did he want to accept any position that would carry with it the least bit of notoriety, and thereby declined.

Cole Younger
Photo Courtesy of the Library of Congress.

An article in the *Springfield Republican* on May 5, 1903, after a grand jury brought Ames' crimes to light, suggested that thoughtful men did not respect him. Ames' moral quality was defined as "flabby." The story further claimed that Ames' liberal views gave him the support of the easy-going and thoughtless criminal voters who remained oblivious of his unlawful operations until circumstances compelled them to look at their man and his organization of law-breaking police officers. The article went on to say that Mayor Ames was the head of a rogue band of officials who made the city of Minneapolis a paradise for criminals, thieves, gamblers and bawdy houses. The writer concluded that Minneapolis was, therefore, an undesirable residence for decent people and in need of a real revival of civic watchfulness.

Ames found himself in hot water for a number of crimes. One involved the solicitation of a $1,000 bribe from J.C. Sodini, proprietor of the Columbia Theater. The arrangement was engineered by "Coffee John" Fitchette who secured the check from Sodini. The check was eventually presented as evidence to the grand jury. The bribe was payment for Ames to close down Sodini's competition, a string of variety shows owned by Peter Blar.

Once his theaters were shut down, Blar approached Mayor Ames and asked him what he would take to let him re-open his theaters. They settled on a price of $600. Sodini was outraged by the breach of agreement and appeared at the city offices in a fury, accusing Ames of breaking their contract. Ames took offense and advised Sodini he was lucky to still be alive. Ames threatened to run him out of town if he made a fuss. Sodini turned to the grand jury and the resulting bribery scandal led to six indictments against Ames and, later, to an indictment against Sodini himself for bribing a public official.

Another accusation filed against Ames was grounded in his attempt to bribe county commissioners so his secretary, T. R. Brown, could be elected sheriff. Former Sheriff Philip Megaarden was removed for malfeasance and accepting money from dissolute women. Accused with Ames was his brother, Col. Frederick W. Ames, Superintendent of Police, for accepting a bribe. Some of the others indicted included Captain N. W. King for grand larceny and accessory to felony; Detectives J. C. Howard, John E. Morrissey and Christopher Norbeck and Special Officer Irwin A Gardner for asking and receiving bribes; and Captain George E. Harvey for perjury and asking for a bribe.

Ames fled the Twin Cities hoping to escape prosecution, but was eventually tracked down by Minneapolis detectives. Though thrown off his track in Boston, the detectives stumbled upon a lead that he had reportedly traveled to Louisburg, Kentucky, and West Baden, Indiana, before seeking refuge in New Hampshire. The February 18, 1903, *Plain Dealer* reported the arrest of Ames, declaring him broken in spirit and a physical wreck, probably beyond recognition. He was discovered hiding in the home of a local Manchester, New Hampshire minister, the Rev. C. H. Chapin. Ames was placed under arrest by Sheriff Doane of Manchester.

He was discovered when Minneapolis Police Chief J. W. Greger asked Doane to see if Ames had sought refuge at the home of his sister-in-law. The former mayor suggested he would have returned to Minnesota to face the music on his own had he been a well man, but considered himself on the verge of collapse. According to the newspaper article:

> "Dr. Ames is wonderfully changed from the description of him sent out by the Minneapolis police after his disappearance from that city. He has grown a full beard and his hair is almost white. It is said he is sixty-two years of age, but he looks over seventy. His flesh is much wasted away and from a physical standpoint he is helpless."

Ames immediately contacted United States District Attorney Charles J. Hamblett of Nashua to obtain his services in an unsuccessful fight against extradition to Minnesota. Ames was eventually returned to Minneapolis to face his crimes. His defense alleged his crimes were the result of alcoholism, insanity and paresis. The mayor was sentenced to six years in prison, but the decision was overturned on appeal after two mistrials.

He disappeared from Minneapolis and ended up serving no jail time. Ames eventually returned to the city and finished the remainder of his days practicing medicine. He passed away on November 16, 1911, at the age of 69 and his cremated remains are buried at Lakewood Cemetery in Minneapolis. His brother, Fred, became prisoner #1093 in the Stillwater

State Prison and is also buried in the family plot at Lakewood Cemetery.

Hovey C. Clark, head of the 1902 grand jury, is the man credited with bringing the Ames administration to justice

A Finger in Every Pie

Wilber B. Foshay in parade celebrating the completion of the Foshay Tower. Photo courtesy of the W Hotel, Minneapolis.

"Never has an investor of the company lost any money. All your money – All the time – On time."

Wilbur B. Foshay's Marketing Slogan

The March 22, 1929, *Seattle Daily Times* carried a headline claiming, "If There's a Pie Anywhere, Foshay's Finger Is in It!" The article reported that Wilber B. Foshay was in Seattle on business with the goal of adding to his vast, multi-national holdings. The paper announced that Foshay was traveling with three secretaries who "count many baskets for his financial eggs." The problem—the eggs in Foshay's baskets didn't belong to him.

Foshay, then known as a world-class promoter, built a monument to white collar crime when he erected the Foshay Tower. The building holds a historic place in downtown Minneapolis. Today guests can stay at the revamped Foshay, now operating as the W Hotel, and bask in the lap of luxury while taking in the city's highlights. Back then, Foshay left the city with a skyscraper built on the fast and loose regulations enjoyed by the financial industry leading up to the Great Depression of the 1930s.

A portly, well-liked gentleman, Foshay was a marketing genius with the cunning of a flimflam man. Originally from Ossining, New York, Foshay studied art, electricity and engineering at the Cooper Institute and the Massachusetts Technical Institute in Boston as a young man. He held numerous positions in the public utilities field throughout the country and purchased his first utility company in Hutchinson, Kansas. Foshay landed in Minnesota in 1914 at the age of 36 and built a financial house of cards from his offices at 828-830 Second Avenue South in Minneapolis.

Foshay and his wife, Leota Hutchinson Foshay, along with their children, William and Julianne, attended St. Mark's Episcopal Church in the Loring Park neighborhood. Foshay was also a member of the Minneapolis Athletic Club, the Lafayette Club, the Benevolent Order of the Elks and Masonic fraternity. He was a keen supporter of the Boy Scouts of America.

With a $6,000 unsecured loan, Foshay created the Foshay Company and began purchasing telephone, gas and electric power companies. These included utilities in Minnesota and surrounding states. He financed his purchases by selling Foshay securities in a well-constructed Ponzi scheme. With the liberal financial regulations in place during the 1920s, individuals could borrow money to purchase Foshay's stock using only the stock's value as collateral.

Foshay's final purchases included a chain of utilities in Canada, Nicaragua, Honduras and Mexico. He also owned three Twin Cities banks and subsidiary businesses in 30 states such as wholesale and retail drug stores, hotel companies, food and textile factories, rubber factories, flour mills and retail furniture stores.

In 1926, the officers of the Foshay Company, who were determined to have complete control over operations, offered holders of common stock (stock which gave the stockholder a vote in affairs of the company) two shares of preferred stock for every single share of common stock. This enabled the officers to retire $100,000 in voting shares, giving them complete control of the company. This control allowed Foshay Company officers the opportunity to pay themselves large salaries. Foshay's average annual salary over thirteen years was $53,000.

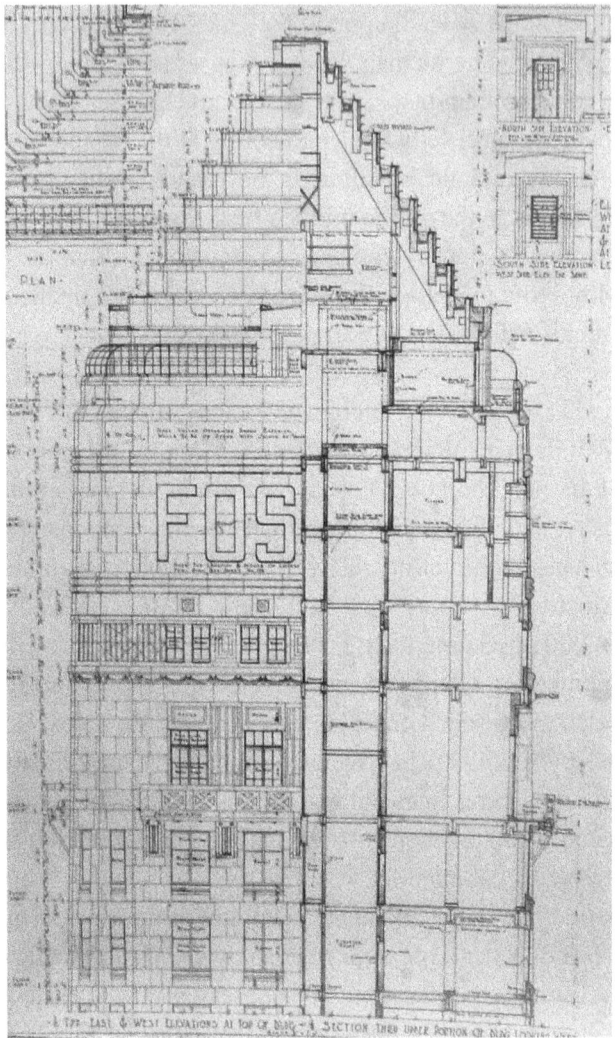

Blueprint of the Foshay Tower.
Courtesy of the W Hotel, Minneapolis.

In one year, Foshay paid himself $306,000 in salaries and bonuses. H. H. Henley, his business partner, averaged nearly $36,000.

Foshay began selling his securities to the public in the East, employing an army of salesmen and amassing $22,000,000 in just ten years. He celebrated his success by commissioning the Foshay Tower, a thirty-two story structure shaped like the Washington Monument and rising to over 447 feet above street level from a larger square base two stories in height. It was to be located at 821-37 Marquette Avenue in Minneapolis. When completed, it would be the tallest skyscraper west of the Mississippi.

The 27th and 28th floors of the building were to be his place of business and his residence, sporting three bedrooms and baths, with a fireplace, library, Italian Sienna marbled walls and glass paneled ceilings. However, he and his family would never occupy the space.

An article printed in *The New York Times,* dated August 25, 1929, called the new Foshay Tower a dedication to Washington. The grand opening guest list included dignitaries from Washington D.C. and several Canadian provinces; governors of all fifty states; and the presidents of Honduras and Nicaragua. The celebration lasted for three days.

Foshay commissioned renowned composer and patriot John Philip Sousa to write a rousing march for the price of $20,000. The march was entitled the *Foshay Tower Washington Memorial* and was performed by Sousa's band. Foshay reportedly spent $116,000 on the celebration. Twenty-five thousand guests were invited to the event where half-nude women danced as entertainment and each guest received a gold pocket watch.

The celebrating public did not realize Foshay's fortune was the product of smoke and mirrors. Checks began to bounce, including the one for $20,000 issued to Sousa. As a result, Sousa refused to let the march be played again until the debt was paid. In 1988, a group of investors from Minnesota repaid the debt to Sousa's estate, freeing up the march to be performed. A rendition of the march can be heard today at the Foshay Tower Museum on the 30th floor, which also provides access to the observation deck.

Two months after Foshay's over-the-top celebration, the most devastating Wall Street crash in history shook the country. Foshay's companies had an estimated value of $20,000,000, but his liabilities were $19,000,000, not including the $29,000,000 in securities sold to the public. Foshay had flown a banner declaring "Never has an investor of the company lost any money. All your money – All the time – On time."

The men heading the Foshay Company had prior experience working for the largest utility companies in the nation. They regularly wrote up, or appreciate, the company's capital account, implying their companies were of greater value than they actually were. Red warning flags began popping up for the Commerce Commission of the State of Minnesota. The commission denied the company the right to sell $1,000,000 in additional shares of preferred stock because, it said, the company's holdings were too scattered to permit economical operation by the holding company. Additionally, commissioners claimed that the values of the property and stock turned over to Public Utilities Consolidated Corporation were not sufficient to support the proposed capitalization. Lastly, the earnings of the respective operating companies did not justify the proposed capitalization and the holding company. The Commerce Commission, in denying the application for the registration, expressed the opinion that the sale of these securities would "work a fraud on the purchasers thereof."

By December, 1928, the Foshay Company employed 151 full-time, and thirty part-time, salesmen selling Foshay securities. Between 1921 and 1929, they sold 63,895,521 securities. Foshay's salesmen were instructed to point out that these securities were "Foshay managed," supposedly making them safer than an alternative security.

In reality, Foshay was running a pyramid scheme. For instance, in 1920 the net income earned was $2,999, yet the dividends paid were $5,293. The following year, the net income was $7,003 and dividends were paid in the amount of $11,901. Between 1920 and 1929, the Foshay Company paid $1,104,995 in dividends.

The company's accountant testified in court that dividends were paid every year out of either selling stock or from borrowed money. Dividends were paid even while the company was losing money. In addition, Foshay exercised the unusual policy of selling securities with which to purchase property after a contract had been signed with the seller. He was "selling securities in advance of delivery."

The usual method of procedure followed by the Foshay Company was to purchase either the stock, or in some cases, both stock and physical properties of an operating company, appreciate its value, then sell it to a holding company. The appreciation in the case of disposals to Public

Utilities Consolidated Corporation amounted to $2,696,228.

In addition to salesmen promoting the soundness of investing with him, Foshay came up with the idea of purchasing small town newspapers with which to mold his readers' minds. He believed that with 200 – 300 newspapers, he and his business partner, Henley, could control the country's policies because readers elect officials. The plans could not be carried out, brought up short by the company's demise.

The idea of Foshay owning Minnesota and North Dakota newspapers did not sit well with R. F. Pack, vice president and general manager of the Northern States Power Company, leading to a heated exchange of letters. Foshay loved publicity. In 1928, one year before its great fall, the Foshay Company secured 660,000 lines of newspaper publicity, a value claimed at $2,310,000 and counted as company profit.

The reason of the failure was over-expansion, depreciation, creative bookkeeping and ego. Foshay's company went into receivership, to be managed by Merchant-Banker Joseph Chapman.

Paying the Piper

Charges were brought against Foshay and Henley after stockholders lost millions of dollars in investments. Judge J. W. Woodrow with the Federal Court of Appeals termed the situation "merely a dishonest scheme." According to the November 14, 1933, edition of *The New York Times*, the judge explained:

> "People buy shares in corporations to share in their earnings and these appellants always made the representation that Foshay companies had had, and would continue to have, large earnings, and would pay and continue to pay large dividends on their stock."

In March 1934, Foshay and Henley were ordered to surrender within thirty days to start serving fifteen-year sentences in Leavenworth Penitentiary. Meanwhile, Berry Ervin, the head of a committee from Minneapolis seeking leniency for the men, presented a petition to President Franklin Roosevelt seeking executive clemency. He asked that the two be either pardoned or placed on probation, claiming there was no fraudulent intent at any time made by either Foshay or Henley. Similar petitions were also being circulated in Wisconsin and Arizona.

On January 27, 1937, Attorney General Homer Stille Cummings announced that President Roosevelt had commuted the sentences of Foshay and Henley, making them eligible for immediate parole. Cummings said the commutation was the result of hundreds of letters asking for the men's sentences to be reduced. Ten years later, on June 27, 1947, the Justice Department announced that President Harry S. Truman had granted a pardon to Foshay. But the story doesn't have a happy ending for everyone.

Casualties of the Crime

In a strange and tragic twist, a former employee and her family became casualties of Foshay and Henley's crime. Genevieve A. Clark had been found guilty of criminal contempt with attempt to obstruct justice and knowingly misled others in her qualifications as a juror for the Foshay and Henley case. Court records show that when she was summoned to be a juror, she called her sister, (court records did not record the sister's first name) Mrs. Brown, and told her she would prefer not to serve. Her sister checked with the clerk of court, and was advised that any excuses would have to be presented to the judge.

Shortly after that, Clark was advised she would probably not be called to serve on the Foshay and Henley case due to the fact that she had been employed by the Foshay Company. However, on the day of the trial, when she and her husband went to the courtroom for the district judge to examine her as to her qualifications to serve on the jury, Clark told several women that she wished to serve on the jury. For this she had a special reason. She admitted that she had worked for the Foshay Company as a stenographer for about two weeks in the summer of 1929, but had never met either of the defendants.

In addition, she had worked as an assistant cashier at a St. Paul bank where her husband was then president and where Foshay banked. Daniel D. Clark resigned from his bank position in 1925, but continued a business relationship with Foshay. Letters gathered for Mrs. Clark's appeal showed a warm and almost intimate relationship between the two men. When called to the jury box under questioning by the judge, Clark was asked if she had ever been in business of any kind. She admitted that she had been a stenographer before her marriage, going on to say she also worked in a bank, a real estate and insurance company, and was with an automobile concern with a Nash agency. She convinced the judge that her mind was clear of bias and that the law and evidence would govern her arrival at a verdict. She was accepted on the jury

During the eight-week trial, Clark mentioned to other jurors that she saw Foshay as the victim of circumstances. She told them that he had gone to New York in the fall of 1929 to borrow $18,000,000, but that because of the market crash, he came home penniless. During jury deliberations, Clark announced that since the prosecutor could not convince her of wrongdoing, she couldn't see how the others could find him guilty. When the jurors tried to reason with her, she put her hands over her ears and refused to reply to their comments.

She informed the other jurors that the witness for the government, C. M. Coble, an Omaha accountant, had once given perjured evidence in an attempt to convict an innocent man in a previous trial. This information was given to her by her husband in front of the bailiff when he visited her in the hotel where the jury was staying. Due to Clark's refusal to agree with her fellow jurors, the jury was discharged with eleven of the twelve votes finding Foshay and Henley guilty.

On November 4, 1931, the government filed a case against Clark, arguing that her answers upon the voir dire examination by the judge were:

> "Willfully and corruptly false, and that the effect of her misconduct had been to hinder and obstruct the trial. In response to the rule to show cause, the defendant filed an answer denying the misconduct, and alleging that her vote for acquittal had been dictated by her conscience."

The court concluded that:

> "The only plausible explanation is a preconceived endeavor to uphold the cause of the defendants and save them from their doom."

Clark was sentenced to six months in prison and a $1,000 fine. The severe sentence was too much for the Clarks. *Time* magazine carried the following article in its May 8, 1933, Milestone Section:

> Died. Mrs. Genevieve A. Clark, her husband Daniel, their sons Rowland, 10, and Dean, 7; by their own hands (carbon monoxide); on a country road 15 mi. south of Minneapolis. The crash of Wilbur Burton Foshay's Northwestern utilities empire in 1929 brought him & associates, two years later, Federal charges of using the mails to defraud. After an eight-week trial. Mrs. Clark, only woman member of the jury, hung the case by singly holding out for acquittal (TIME, Nov. 2, 1931).* Convicted of contempt of court for concealing the fact that she had once worked for Foshay (two weeks as a stenographer), she was sentenced to six months in jail, a $1,000 fine. (Attorneys found no U. S. precedent involving a woman juror, few sentences so severe for similarly guilty male jurors.) U. S. Circuit and Supreme Courts ruled that she must receive either jail sentence or fine, not both. Last fortnight two St. Paul judges chose jail, ordered Mrs. Clark to begin her term one day last week. She did not appear. Three days later a farmer found the Clark family's bodies huddled in their tightly-shut automobile, a hose in from the exhaust pipe.

Once released from Leavenworth, Foshay and his wife, Leota, moved to Salida, Colorado. That community had a job waiting for him after the town's vigorous letter writing campaign moved President Franklin Roosevelt to commute Foshay's sentence. In the early 1930s, the construction of the Denver & Rio Grande Western Railroad negatively affected the community's businesses. It lost two mines and roughly three thousand residents moved out of Salida. Foshay was hired by the Salida Chamber of Commerce as their paid secretary and, using his God-given gift for promotion, he immediately erected strings of hearts along the highway advising travelers to "Follow the hearts to Salida – the heart of the Rockies."

His biggest promotional hit by far was a claim of "fur-bearing trout" which was so outrageous that it made the newsreels. A search online today for "fur-bearing fish" will bring up articles, many of which include the mention of Foshay. Foshay and his wife lived happily in Salida on an income of $150 a month.

He was loved by his community, going by the nickname of Cap. His efforts proved to be successful and, in 1940, after four years with the Chamber of Commerce, the population of Salida was back to its previous count. It was a way for Foshay to give back to a community that supported him. He was reminded of his past glory by a photograph of the Foshay Tower hanging on the wall of his office and a plaque with the motto:

"Why worry? It won't last. Nothing does."

CHAPTER 2
PROHIBITION

Mr. X's Book Arrives

Dear Elizabeth,

Congratulations! You made history!! I went to the Downtown Minneapolis Public Library (Special Collections Section) and they will now be buying your book to be a <u>permanent</u> part of the library. I also understand they will be ordering more copies to be on their check out shelf! Finally real history (besides "Easy Street," written by gangster Dave Berman's daughter) is going on the shelf!

The four books that I am written about are fun, but just yellow journalism. However, you will enjoy the book I mailed. I'll call you in early September to meet. I look forward to it.

Sincerely,
Mr. X

I received the book mentioned in X's letter and found it quite different from what I imagined. I shouldn't have been surprised. Every generation of gangsters was raised under social and economic conditions different from the one before. If not for a new generation of bank robbers and kidnappers like John Dillinger and Baby Face Nelson, the St. Paul O'Connor system of granting free haven to crime figures might still exist.

The book began with a brief background of Minnesota's first gangsters, like Doc Ames and Kid Cann, and then eventually rolled around to the boys who were coming of age during the 1950s and 60s.
Minneapolis Mayor Hubert Humphrey had already cleaned house, a task begun with culling corrupt members from the city's police force. Organized crime, after all, cannot succeed without the complicity of upstanding members of society.

The book introduced me to the "Baldies," clean-cut young men who wore their hair short. Dressed like Kid Cann wannabes, they distinguished themselves from the "Greasers" or "Animals," a gang with slicked-back hair and attired in blue jeans and leather jackets. The Baldies designed themselves to be the perfect nemesis of their rivals.

"Society prepares the crime, the criminal commits it"

Henry Thomas Buckle

Organized Crime and Prohibition

Sheriff Earle Brown Smashing a Still. Photo courtesy of the Hennepin County Library, Minneapolis Collection, M2714.

"Prohibition makes a crime out of things that are not crimes ... A prohibition law strikes a blow at the very principles upon which our government was founded."

Abraham Lincoln, 1840

    Prior to the Eighteenth Amendment prohibiting the production and transportation of liquor into the United States beginning in 1920, organized crime members made plans with international whiskey manufacturers and politicians to exploit U.S. citizens. The British had a long history of providing America with alcohol through the Hudson Bay Company. The company stocked trading posts throughout North America, first introducing liquor to the Native people.

    Shortly before liquor prohibition went into effect, American liquor was exported to the Bahamas. There it filled warehouses and empty offices and was stacked in the streets beside British liquor awaiting illegal import again into the U.S.

    American organized crime figures built and lived in stucco palaces on the islands.

    The Baltimore American reported on August 8, 1921, that American dry laws made it possible for the Bahaman Islands, an archipelago of the British Empire, to pay off public debt via import liquor transactions, thus lifting the formerly bankrupt Nassauvians out of poverty. Winston Churchill refused to apologize for breaking U.S. laws or to take any restrictive action while the Eighteenth Amendment extracted wealth from the United States and into British coffers.

American Charles Murphy operated a Bahamas-based liquor exporting business, the Bahama Islands Import and Export Company, which provided Americans with American whiskey. He was considered as near to a political boss of the Bahamas as possible. The U.S. State Department, informed with regular reports from Lorin A. Lathorp, the American Consul at Nassau, was fully aware of the situation in the Bahamas. Prior to his assignment in Nassau, Lathorp served as a diplomat in Bristol, England, from 1902 to 1914. He had close ties to the British government.

While Congress could have allowed the brewing industry to continue employing Americans in the production of liquor, making it illegal to sell domestically but legal to export, the United States' version made it illegal to produce alcohol at all. According to one school of thought, the oil industry wanted to discourage the production of grain alcohol, declared by Henry Ford as the future of the auto industry. The amendment did not, however, make the consumption of alcohol illegal. Those with stocks of liquor were able to retain them as long as they were not transporting or selling that alcohol. Any doctor, lawyer, politician, or pauper with a cellar full of liquor could imbibe in peace. The result of this careful crafting of legislation was the creation of a huge black market.

A treaty signed in the early 1920s by the United States, Canada and Great Britain allowed liquor to be brought into U.S. territorial waters on passenger ships. The U.S. Coast Guard could stop and search a ship suspected as a rum runner within an hour of shore. From just outside the designated territory, liquor was unloaded onto smaller boats from mostly British ships. From there organized crime transported the alcohol to various harbors, typically off the Florida coast and New England states, for sale on the black market.

On April 20, 1923, in Great Britain, Member of Parliament Edwin Scrymgeour addressed his country's role in providing the United States with illegal liquor in a speech to the House of Commons:

> "On that point I am bound to say that it is a matter for astonishment to me that people in this country who profess to be constitutionalists and upholders of law and order should have, in newspapers, in public utterances and as Members of this House, appeared to gloat over this lawbreaking in America and its results. I say it is disgraceful, and I say more than that. We are told in the columns of the constitutionalist Press that hundreds of thousands of gallons of whisky are shipped from this country to the Bahamas and elsewhere for illicit importation to America.
>
> That can only be done with the connivance of the great whisky manufacturers in this country, some of whom sit in the House of Lords..."

Criminals and Politicians were Ready

In 1916, Sam and Harry Bronfman opened a retail liquor outlet in Montreal and built stills and small hotels in Winnipeg near the Minnesota-Canadian border. The family, known today for its ownership of Seagram's liquor and its generous philanthropy, looked into the future and saw dollar signs. The Bronfmans developed working relationships with organized crime figures from Canada, like Abe Goldman and Harry Rabinovitch, as well as those located in the Twin Cities such as Michael Weisman, Kid Cann and Tommy Banks. In Minneapolis, public officials provided cover to the criminals, working hand-in-hand to carry out crimes.

At the end of Prohibition, the United States Government claimed Canadian distillers owed $60,000,000 in excise and customs taxes on alcohol shipments. The Canadians finally agreed to pay $3,000,000 with the Bronfmans putting up half of the payment.

When Prohibition went into effect in 1920, Minneapolis criminals and compliant politicians had already been working together in the smuggling trade. They moved Canadian whiskey, which had been exported to the U.S during Canada's bout with prohibition, back into Canada and onto the black market. Canadians liked drinking Canadian whiskey.

In Minneapolis, William M. (Bud) Nash began his term as Hennepin

County Attorney on the first Monday in January 1919. Just a little over a year later, on May 17, 1920, George B. Safford, head of the Anti-Saloon League, petitioned Governor Joseph A. A. Burnquist to remove Nash and Hennepin County Sheriff Oscar Martinson from office on the grounds of malfeasance in the performance of their duties.

Hennepin County Attorney Bud Nash.
Photo courtesy of the Hennepin County Library.

The pair was accused of receiving bribes from bootlegger Michael Weisman who bought the protection of certain individuals in the commission of bootlegging crimes. Nash apparently struck a bargain to protect Sheriff Martinson, Weisman and nine others (three holding the title of county deputy) as they received, transported and concealed large quantities of liquor imported from the Dominion of Canada. In the first three months of 1920, federal agents estimated that around twenty carloads of whiskey, valued at more than $1,000,000, had been shipped into Minnesota from Canada.

On May 11, 1920, Nash and Martinson were arrested on suspicion of conspiracy to receive, conceal and facilitate the transportation of whiskey into Minnesota from Winnipeg, Canada. The charges were made after

Weisman and co-conspirator, Frank Bank, entered guilty pleas and explained to law enforcement how the system worked.

Weisman described the arrangement Nash had with the bootleggers:

Governor J.A.A. Burnquist.
Photo courtesy of the Hennepin County Library.

Nash would remain in his office at night during the unloading of liquor shipped from Canada so that, if an individual was arrested, he would be available to have the bootlegger promptly released from jail. Weisman paid Nash handsomely for this service. Weisman initially offered Nash $200 for this protection but, according to the bootlegger, Nash said he "wouldn't sit in his office five minutes for $200." He wouldn't take less than $1,000, which Weisman retrieved from his own bank vault and paid in $100 bills. In addition, Sheriff Martinson was paid $200.

Attorney Nash was also accused of a rash of illegal activity including a payment of $2,000 from Weisman to use his official position to merely fine four women accused of running a house of ill-repute rather than send them to jail.

At the time of their arrests, Weisman had paid Nash $11,800 in bribes.

Liquor Heist at the Soo Rail Yard

Early in 1920, shortly after Prohibition went into effect, Sheriff Martinson, and six Twin Cities businessmen attempted to pull off the greatest liquor smuggling case up until that date. Five coal cars with false bottoms were brought in from Canada loaded with $150,000 worth of liquor covered with scrap iron. The illegal shipment was under the protection of the Hennepin County Sheriff's Office. Federal agents, working under the direction of T. E Campbell, eventually served warrants on the local men who broke the Reed Amendment prohibiting the shipment of intoxicating liquor in interstate commerce.

At another time, Harry Rabinovitch, an organized crime member from Winnipeg, attempted to rob a railway car of cases of his own whiskey on its way from St. Louis to Winnipeg. Rabinovitch was associated with the Regina Wine and Spirits Company owned by the Bronfman family. In 1921, Michael Weisman testified for the government in the liquor conspiracy case tried before Judge Wilbur F. Booth. He explained the nature of the transaction while his attorney, E.S. Cary, stood by.

The whiskey was bought in Chicago by Abe Goldberg and Harry Rabinovitch with the intention of shipping it to, and unloading it in, Minneapolis. If that plan failed, they intended to send the whiskey on to Winnipeg, consigned to the Canadian Wine & Spirits Company owned by Harry Rabinovitch. Weisman was unable to provide necessary protection for the planned delivery in Minneapolis.

He went on to describe how he contacted his brother-in-law who was working for a railroad yard but "found there was nothing doing in that direction." He knew no other railroad men. Rabinovitch said he was going to have the railway car pushed into St. Paul that night. A ring of Twin Cities businessmen set to purchase and distribute the liquor had already deposited $13,000 in a St. Paul bank for the first payment.

Weisman drove to St. Paul in an automobile owned by Sheriff Martinson and met Rabinovitch at the St. Paul Hotel. Rabinovich wanted $38,000 in advance of delivery, so sought out C. H. Couplin, a pawnbroker who promised the money upon receipt of the whiskey and not before. Weisman returned to the pawnbroker's store the next morning when someone entered and said, "If any of you boys are interested in that whiskey car you'd better duck. There's been a killing."

Soo Line Engine in Minneapolis rail yard.
Photo courtesy of the Hennepin County Library.

During the unloading of the whiskey the night before, St. Paul prize fighter and pugilist Jack Burke was shot and killed. Albert Spiess from 727 Rondo Street described the attempted heist. He was a driver for Ed M. Holton and had driven Holton's limousine to the Soo rail yard while W.J. Ueber drove a light Dodge truck up to the whiskey car. Speiss, under his employer's direction, jumped into the whiskey car in an attempt to unload the cases. Burke, Holton, Ueber and Spiess were unloading the rail car when a vehicle appeared at the far end of the yard.

Spiess had time to hand out just four cases of liquor when someone directed Burke to tell the men to put out the lights on their cars. Burke managed to turn the lights of one car out and was headed toward a second vehicle when shooting erupted. Spiess leapt from the rail car and raced around to the end with the gunmen shooting and in close pursuit. He scrambled over a pile of lumber, dropping twenty-five feet down the opposite side. His pursuers, hesitant to jump, stood atop the lumber pile shooting at him in the darkness.

Additional testimony of the conspiracy came from yardmaster Frank S. Luxem of Gary, Indiana. He explained that Soo line freight agent George L. Morrison had advised him to keep it under his hat that a car of liquor was coming over from Minneapolis and was to be "touched up" that night. Luxem was told:

> "It is not going to be robbed, but a couple of hundred cases of the liquor are going to be taken out by the owner. The company is fully protected. There will be no claim made by the owner for the shortage of goods. It is all up to the special agents who are officers of the government."

When Attorney Nash became aware that his office and the sheriff's office were to be investigated by the grand jury, he asked the judge of the district court for removal of a grand juror deemed especially influential in the investigation.

On the day of his hearing, Sheriff Martinson went to court without an attorney and admitted his guilt:

> "The statement I have made is absolutely true. I have been a public official and erred in my duty."

At the conclusion of the trial, Martinson was sentenced to two years in Fort Leavenworth prison. He collapsed as he was leaving the stand after testifying and remained unconscious for half an hour. Earle Brown, farmer and local real estate man, was then appointed sheriff of Hennepin County on May 14, 1920, to replace the disgraced Martinson.

Of the case, Judge Page Morris commented:

> " I fear the court has taken a birds-eye view to discern the rottenness of this case, but simply from the testimony I should say there is a horrible condition in Hennepin County. Every time a carload of whiskey is brought in from Canada it is guarded by the deputy sheriffs. Officials elected by the people to guard the public's interest, it appears are in league with the wrongdoers. It is a horrible, horrible condition."

Appearing somewhat proud of the significance of the crime, a coterie of Minneapolis aldermen led by J. B. Ryan toured a number of Eastern cities in May of 1920 collecting information and ideas from communities

Hennepin County Courtroom Number One.
Photo courtesy of the Hennepin County Library.

about the construction of public auditoriums, comfort stations and municipal markers. They boasted to the *Philadelphia Enquirer* that the recent $25,000 Philadelphia transit graft scandal looked like "small town stuff" compared to the Minneapolis crime. "We're having a hefty little chunk of publicity on our own account as a result."

Government complicity in crimes appeared to be second nature in Minneapolis with officials needing to be replaced from time to time. Although he voted as a Democrat and later as a member of the Farmer-Labor party, Floyd B. Olson was promoted from assistant county attorney to county attorney in the Republican administration by former Lieutenant Governor of Minnesota "Big Ed" Smith, the Republican boss.

Nash's removal from office appeared to have little effect on his career as an attorney. He was later acquitted under appeal. His firm, Nash and Nichols, continued to work closely with County Attorney Olson on many criminal trials, securing an impressive record of significantly-reduced sentences and dismissed cases

CHAPTER 3
A SOFT SPOT FOR RACKETEERING

Photo Album

 I met with Mr. X again at "our" place. He brought a promised garbage bag full of photo albums to the restaurant. We didn't eat pizza this time, though he remembered my penchant for brownies and treated me to one. He wanted to keep the table clear for photos. I knew this ahead of time because Mr. X tends to orchestrate things. I just follow his lead. I really enjoyed perusing the photographs, even though I didn't know the people in them, except, of course, the mobster sitting across from me.
 Mr. X's life appeared surprisingly ordinary with a lovely, wholesome-looking wife (too wholesome, he said) and several beautiful children who seemed quite fond of their dad. Only a yacht in one of the photos distinguished this family photo album from albums familiar to me.
 Then we got to the images of the Baldies. Deuce Casper stood, hands in pockets, laughing. Mr. X said the cops, not the gang members, named the gang. I viewed photos of other Baldies, some of them now dead.
 The album also included many photos of Mr. X's former lover, who

morphed into an old woman as we turned the pages. She is now his best friend. His current lover is beautiful and much younger and smiles brightly at the camera.

I savored walking down memory lane with Mr. X, sensing his pride in once belonging to the biggest, baddest gang in Minneapolis' colorful history and, yet, shaking his head at some of their antics. He patiently answered my questions about the order of organized crime in the Twin Cities, as I tried to follow the mob's lineage from pre-Kid Cann to present day organized crime. "Disorganized is more like it," Mr. X said, quoting a current mob member. "Disorganized?" Now what is that supposed to mean.

Mr. X, a bit of a philosopher, likes talking about this stuff. He confesses without apology: "I am an old man, still in love with my sins."

1920 -1930s

Conspiracy:
An agreement between two or more persons to engage jointly in an unlawful or criminal act, or an act that is innocent, in and of itself, but becomes unlawful when done by the combination of actors.

The Free Dictionary

Minneapolis Racketeering

Minneapolis was known as a "soft spot" for racketeering. Underworld crimes took place daily and newspaper reporters knew the facts, but soft-pedaled them for fear that negative press would hurt the city's reputation and be bad for business.

A headline from the February 8, 1936, *New York Times* announced "Politicians Linked to Twin Cities Gangs – Investigator Reports Minneapolis is Divided into Racket Districts by Thugs." The article describes, within the "political structure," a far-flung vice and crime network whose existence was underscored by the murder of two investigative journalists within two years. Newspaperman Walter Liggett's murder trial was in progress when H. G. Benton, secretary of the Minneapolis Real Estate Board, presented an investigator's report commissioned by the realty board. The organization brought in out-of-state investigator J.M. Simmons.

The investigative results were announced in a radio address by Charles W. Drews, executive secretary of the Minneapolis Law and Order League, as he explained that the findings would be turned over to a grand jury. The report described the underworld gangs' arrangements within the city as a sharing of territory in which gambling existed and in which two brothers, Davie and "Chickie" Berman, controlled prostitution concession trafficking between Minneapolis and St. Paul. Israel "Ice Pick Willie" Alderman served as trafficking enforcer. Other major underworld figures included Isadore "Kid Cann" Blumenfield and Tommy Banks. The arrangement, the report suggested, could not be possible without the compliance of local politicians and law enforcement.

Rather than applaud the work of the investigator, or compliment the initiative of the Minneapolis Law and Order League in trying to stomp

Mayor Thomas Latimer (1935–39).
Photo courtesy of the Hennepin County Library.

out organized crime, Mayor Thomas Latimer instead took a defensive stance, stating:

> "I challenge Mr. Simmons to present evidence, if he has any – which I seriously doubt – to the city attorney or the grand jury."

Likewise, Police Chief Frank Forestal termed the report "ridiculous." Still, as the Liggett trial went on and underworld figure Isadore Blumenfield's attorney tried to establish his innocence through an ironclad alibi, three bankers and one policeman testified on behalf of Blumenfield.

Another *New York Times* article, from February 9, 1936, announced "Grand Jury Eyes Minnesota Crime."

> "There's enough stuff here to keep us busy until next December,"

Hennepin County Grand Jury Foreman Oliver T. Naugle is quoted as saying. The article also noted a running feud between Governor Floyd B. Olson and Colonel Robert R. McCormick, publisher of the Chicago Tribune. In that story, McCormick appears to hold Olson accountable for Liggett's death.

At the Mayo Clinic in Rochester, Minnesota, Olson was being treated for the stomach cancer which would eventually kill him. From his hospital room, Olson blasted McCormick, accusing him of being "a czaristic-minded reactionary" and a "journalistic charlatan." He went on to suggest that "Chicago was a cesspool of corruption and crime." Olson also said McCormick was morally responsible for the deaths of individuals from dysentery during the 1933 World's Fair because he had suppressed the truth.

While speaking in Columbus, Ohio, McCormick continued the feud, claiming that "Olson lent aid and assistance to gangland in its campaign of murdering editors and all who cross his path." Olson responded that the charge was false, and Colonel McCormick knew it. "He makes that charge because he hates me for what he calls 'ultra-radicalism.' He is a faker in his alleged championship of the freedom of the press. Dozens of papers have been suppressed because of their economic views without a word from Bertie. It is only when a scandal sheet has difficulty that Bertie comes to the rescue."

Governor Floyd B. Olson working from bed while suffering from stomach cancer. Photo courtesy of the Hennepin County Library.

Governor Floyd B. Olson.
Photo Courtesy of the Hennepin County Library.

Olson had a history of showing leniency with criminals. Years earlier, on November 8, 1921, local organized crime member, Big Mose Barnett, was charged with larceny in the first degree for stealing an automobile. Barnett's attorney pleaded not ready when the case came to trial and Olson granted a delay. Court records show that new hearings were set on eight different occasions, with Olson finally striking the case from the records on January 2, 1924. (Case# 19362 in the criminal files of Hennepin County).

Years later, on the evening of March 25, 1925, Barnett approached businessman Roy Rogers at the corner of Sixth Street and Hennepin Avenue in Minneapolis and shot him. Contrary to what one would expect of a man who had just shot another man at the populous corner of a city street, Barnett made no attempt to escape. He was arraigned the following day in police court, charged with first degree assault and released on $2,000 bail. The case was later dismissed by County Attorney Olson with no effort to try Barnett for attempted murder.

Grain Price Manipulation

"Within the four walls of this new building, business will be transacted which will affect the breadstuffs of the world."

—George A. Pillsbury, 1884
President, Minneapolis Chamber of Commerce

In 1903, the Minneapolis Chamber of Commerce, today referred to as the Minneapolis Grain Exchange, celebrated its move into the finest and most sumptuous grain exchange building in the country at 400 and 412 South Fourth Street and 301 Fourth Avenue South. Founded on October 19, 1881, it eventually became the premiere wheat trading organization in the United States.

H. G. Harrison, a leading banker in Minneapolis, served as the Chamber's first president. His fellow incorporators, with few exceptions, had no direct connection with the grain and flour trade. Two of the organization's earliest founders, and most influential members, were William Wallace Cargill and Frank Hutchinson Peavey. They began buying up grain elevators throughout the region, gaining control of the grain industry. Through their experience, political and social ties, and industrial genius, they enabled the Minneapolis Chamber to corner cereal trading in the region. Though good for the traders, their policies put the farmers, who provided commodities to their enterprises, at an economic disadvantage.

An 1889 article in the *Duluth Daily News* carried an opinion about Minnesota's grain inspection law, which worked in favor of traders but was detrimental to farmers. Minnesota's state grain inspection law was copied from Illinois law, but differed in the appeals process for disagreements in grading of grain. The Illinois law created a board of appeals, comprised of grain experts who could act immediately upon a case. In Minnesota, a single, independent arbitrator considered the appeals and made the calls as he saw them. The article termed Minnesota's appeals process impractical and an impediment to grain traffic. The financial end of the grain market also worked in favor of the few wealthy investors because all elevators in the state were owned by private individuals rather than by the public. That enabled manipulation of profits.

A decidedly conservative institution, the Chamber of Commerce considered itself superior to the former Minneapolis Board of Trade. The Board opposed the Chamber's creation and replacement of the Miller's Association twenty years earlier. The Chamber of Commerce publicly accused the Miller's Association of fixing prices. But it was a case of the pot calling the kettle black as these powerful men would soon face their own allegations of unfair business practices.

Chamber of Commerce building, now known as the Minneapolis Grain Exchange.
Photo courtesy of the Hennepin County Library.

Between 1912 and 1917, the Federal Trade Commission estimated that 70 percent of the region's grain harvest was funneled through Minneapolis. In 1913, the area experienced what was considered one of the biggest battles fought against big business in the history of Minnesota and the Northwest. A Minnesota House investigation committee, formed by the prompting of farmers in Chippewa County, found that the Minneapolis Chamber of Commerce was conspiring with railroads to charge shippers $1.50 per carload of grain. No such charge was made by the railroad company.

In an unprecedented move, a second committee was created in the Senate at the request of the Minneapolis Chamber. It was opened with the assistance of Democratic Senator S. D. Works to start a back-fire on the investigation by the House committee. The Senate committee intended to go after the Farmer's Equity Exchange, an organization based in St. Paul to provide farmers with access to a fair grain market. Grain elevators and mills were also found, through the investigation, to be in complicity with the Chamber.

In addition to implementing arbitrary fees, Chamber members charged farmers' elevators 7 percent interest for money loaned by banks at 5 ½ percent. In return, elevators had to sell all of their grain to the company which loaned them the money, thereby restricting competitive bidding. This kept commodity prices paid to farmers unnaturally low with grain then resold at the higher fair market price. A Chamber member agreed during testimony that option trading at his organization, which was controlled by the line elevators and milling interests, could adversely affect the region's farmers.

Membership in the Chamber was limited by a cost far beyond that affordable by an average grain merchant. Large business concerns, on the other hand, were able to purchase and control as many memberships as desired. Strict rules prohibited members from trading with anyone outside the Chamber; any member doing so faced suspension. Some of the largest businesses, which were owners of commission concerns who bought and sold commodities, sold grain to themselves. The investigating committee reviewed evidence proving that the Chamber was guilty of bribing elevator managers so shippers had control of their products.

Legal counsel representing the Chamber of Commerce was headed by H. V. Mercer, law partner of Senator George P. Wilson, a member of the Senate Grain and Warehouse Committee. Farmers' interests were represented by Benjamin Drake Jr., a leader in the farmers' Non-Partisan

League political party.

Mercer defended the Chamber, suggesting "bucket shops" (Defined by the U.S. Supreme court as "[a]n establishment, nominally for the transaction of a stock exchange business, or business of similar character, but really for the registration of bets, or wagers, usually for small amounts, on the rise or fall of the prices of stocks, grain, oil, etc., there being no transfer or delivery of the stock or commodities nominally dealt in) were responsible for changing quotations to suit themselves and for creating animosity toward the Chamber. The organization, Mercer claimed, was backed by "men of financial responsibility who did business on the square."

At the onset of the investigation, several leading members of the Chamber were suddenly called out of town where they could not be served subpoenas. In their absence, their attorneys fought hard to restrict the amount of evidence made available to the investigating committee and tried hard to keep such information out of the public domain. Despite their efforts, enough information was revealed to give the committee an understanding of illegal Chamber operations.

Adding to the Chamber's woes, the Chicago-based newspaper, *The Day Book*, reported a stir on the Chicago Board of Trade when it learned that almost every new member of the North Dakota legislature elected that year was voted in on an Anti-Board of Trade ticket. North Dakota farmers relied on the Minneapolis Chamber of Commerce to bring their crops to market. The candidates were members of the Non-Partisan League supported by the Farmer's Equity Exchange of St. Paul. The paper reported:

> North Dakota is the principal wheat state of America, and if the farmer-controlled legislature makes laws which will cut wheat pit dealers and commission men out of the gambling and middle-man sales commission an awful hole will be made in the profits of these grain dealers, who are reputed to often make more profit on a bushel of grain than the farmer, miller and storekeeper combined.

On December 9, 1914, Congressman James Manahan made a fiery speech at the Equity Grain Exchange in St. Paul denouncing the Minneapolis Chamber of Commerce as "the most vicious of gambling institutions" before a crowd of 3,500 grain men and farmers, some of whom traveled over a thousand miles to attend. Discussions throughout the day included the creation of cooperative associations between farmers to bring their crops to market without the use of a middleman.

Manahan introduced legislation directing Congress to investigate the boards of trade in Minneapolis, Duluth and Chicago to determine whether they were, in combination, a restraint on trade. He charged the entities with violating the Sherman anti-trust laws by controlling the price of wheat, thus costing farmers and consumers money. It took eight more years before farmers were unshackled from the market forces controlled by the Minneapolis Chamber of Commerce and Chicago

Chamber of Commerce trading room.
Photo courtesy of the Hennepin County Library.

Board of Trade. Their freedom came in the form of the *Capper-Volstead Act* which allowed farmers to create cooperative marketing associations for producers of agricultural products. This act protected cooperatives from antitrust laws and is often referred to as the "Magna Carta" of cooperation.

Deadly Investment

Minneapolis Reverend Knute B. Birkeland, former Lutheran clergyman, author, businessman and head of Augsburg Theological Seminary, believed he was investing in a solid gas and oil company when he bought shares from local attorney Olof Ludwig Bruce, former general manager of the Minneapolis Weekly, a religious and political paper. Instead, he had purchased a one-way ticket to his own murder in a shabby flat at 29 North 12th Street.

Birkeland sued Bruce and his organization for $300,000 for selling fraudulent shares. A hearing was in full swing when Birkeland suddenly disappeared. At the time of the lawsuit, Bruce was in the process of being disbarred by the Minnesota Supreme Court for perjury in connection with the fake company. Birkeland was no rube when it came to investing in energy, making fortunes in whale oil as president of the North Pacific Sea Products Company of Seattle and later in petroleum in Texas.

The plan to dispose of the reverend was elaborate. The intent was to kidnap Birkeland who would then appear to go missing. His failure to appear in court for the fraud suit would result in its dismissal. If all went well, he would be discovered in a house of ill-repute, seriously damaging his reputation. Mayme Hodges, who was later tracked down in Milwaukee, Wisconsin, rented an apartment under the name of Reynolds and furnished it to resemble a massage parlor. The investigation revealed that the murderers had not actually intended to kill Birkeland.

On November 24, 1925, while leaving the Hennepin County Courthouse, the 74-year-old Birkeland was abducted. The medical examiner's report estimated that he passed away on the fourth day of his disappearance while his family searched feverishly for him. One week after he had gone missing, Birkeland's body was discovered by janitors who broke into a flat on 12th Street. Those same janitors testified later that they had observed the unconscious Birkeland being carried into the residence the day he disappeared.

Chief of Police Frank Brunskill.
Photo courtesy of Mark Evans, Midwest American.

Chief Frank Brunskill assigned the murder investigation to chief of detectives, Joseph Lehmeyer, who refused to work with private detectives hired by the family. He also refused to let his own Bertillion expert (named after Alphonse Bertillion, the French policeman who began the practice of using fingerprints to identify criminals and who also invented the mug shot) collect fingerprints at the crime scene. Lehmeyer was accused by Birkeland's family of encouraging people to handle evidence in the apartment. During the hearing, when detective Lehmeyer was asked why he had not allowed fingerprints to be taken, Hennepin Country Attorney Floyd B. Olson interrupted the detective, asserting to the court that fingerprinting was not a science and that no case had ever been solved using fingerprints. "It's just storybook stuff."

Olson announced that his office would take over the investigation and advised the family to "hush up" because it was clear Birkeland had gone to the massage parlor voluntarily where he died of "sexual excitement." He suggested closing the case would be the best way to avoid a scandal in the news.

The family did not, for one moment, believe Olson's version of the story and demanded an inquest and post-mortem examination. The exam, conducted by Dr. E. T. Bell, a member of the staff at the University of Minnesota, revealed that Birkeland had not eaten, nor drunk anything, for four days before his death. This was determined by the condition of the tongue, throat, stomach and bowels.

The defense brought in several women of the evening who ran massage parlors and who perfectly described the victim's appearance, particularly his full beard. A photograph of the victim confirmed their descriptions were accurate. However, the photo was taken years earlier and Birkeland had not sported a beard for several years since. When counsel for the Birkeland family pointed this out to Olson, he said he had additional witnesses who described the victim as clean-shaven.

When the family's attorney began pummeling the second woman with a barrage of questions, she broke down, admitting that Police Chief Brunskill coached her and that she had never met, nor seen, Birkeland. The jury at the inquest could not determine whether the death was by murder or from natural causes.

The family was crestfallen, believing they would receive no justice at the hands of Minneapolis and Hennepin County authorities. They petitioned the help of Governor Theodore Christianson who turned the case over to Attorney General Clifford Hilton, a justice of the State Supreme Court. Quietly, without Olson's knowledge, Hilton issued a warrant for the arrest of Mayme Hodges. The Sheriff immediately went to La Crosse, Wisconsin, where he seized Hodges for extradition. Upon hearing the news, Olson sent investigator Melvin Passolt to Wisconsin to consult with Governor John J. Blaine. Passolt asked the Governor to delay signing the extradition order until Olson had a chance to present the case to the Hennepin County grand jury – in spite of being directed in writing not to do so by the Attorney General.

Olson brought women of the street to testify before the grand jury, yet did not allow family members to tell their side of the story. As a result, the grand jury returned a "no bill"(the term written across the face of a bill of indictment when it has been determined that there is not sufficient evidence to warrant prosecution) in the case of Mayme Hodges. When Governor Blaine received word of the "no bill," he refused to sign the extradition papers and the Hodges woman was released and disappeared.

The Birkeland family had no avenues of justice left. Reverend Birkeland's son began printing a small newspaper charging Police Chief Brunskill with complicity in the murder of his father. After the printing of eight issues of the paper, young Birkeland was arrested, placed on trial for criminal libel and found not guilty.

Campaign Pamphlet Exposes Olson

During the 1920s and 30s, Hennepin County Attorney Floyd B. Olson was suspected of having ties with the criminal element. That rumor took on additional credibility when Ramsey County Attorney C. D. O'Brien issued a flyer during his own campaign for office, unintentionally lending credence to longstanding hearsay. He never used Olson's name, only his statistics. The pamphlet was circulated by the O'Brien Volunteer Committee to Re-Elect C. D. O'Brien.

The document included the following information:

> In Hennepin County 54 percent of those pleading not guilty were dismissed without trial over the three-year period of 1927, 1928 and 1929. In Ramsey County only 12 percent of such cases were dismissed.
>
> In other words, if a criminal pleads not guilty in Hennepin County his chances of escaping trial and being cleared by dismissal are four times as good as they are in Ramsey County.
>
> In Ramsey County, during the three years named, over 94 percent of those accused were either convicted or pleaded guilty. That is only 5 ½ percent of those accused escaped punishment. In Hennepin County during the same period the percentage was 22 percent. In other words, the chances of escaping punishment by pleading not guilty, is four times as good in Hennepin County as in Ramsey County.
>
> During the years 1927, 1928 and 1929 there were 399 criminal cases dismissed in Hennepin County. In Ramsey County there were only 14 such cases dismissed.

The public, dissatisfied with Olson's performance, called for his removal. One of the most noted attempts to have Olson replaced came in 1928, when seven Protestant clergymen and two prominent laymen petitioned Republican Governor Theodore Christianson of Dawson. They formally asked that Olson be suspended as prosecuting attorney of Hennepin County pending a probe by a specially-appointed state investigator selected by the Governor.

The ministers submitted the following request:

The court records indicate that he (Floyd B. Olson) has failed to properly perform the duties of his office to such an extent that we feel it is necessary and timely that the Executive Department of the State intervene for the protection of citizens, the good name of the city of Minneapolis and the safe-guarding of our free institutions.

> REV. CHAS. O. BEMILS, Shiloh-Bethany Presbyterian Comm.
> REV. CLAUDE E. IRELAND, Grace Methodist-Episcopal
> CLAUS MORGAN, Grace Methodist –Episcopal
> E. J. J. SENNETTE, Minnehaha-Nokomis Improvement Assoc.
> REV. H. C. CASPERSON, Lutheran Free Church of America
> GEORGE SVERDRUP, Augsburg Seminary
> OLIN S. REIGSTAD, Bethlehem Lutheran
> T. O. BURNTVEDT, Bethlehem Lutheran
> J.A.O. STUB, Central Lutheran

Governor Christianson ignored the petition.

Government Price Fixing

Investigative journalist Walter Liggett ran newspaper articles in the *Midwest American* accusing Governor Floyd B. Olson of issuing contracts based on politics rather than honest bid-letting. For instance, in 1931, Department of Highways Commissioner Charles Babcock received a letter from newly-elected Governor Olson instructing him to set forth new regulations under which highway contracts would be let. Olson's guidelines limited bidding to contractors who had laid 100,000 square yards of paving the previous year. This new ruling allowed for the collusion of agreements among the six contractors who qualified. The contractors met at the Minneapolis Athletic Club where they agreed to price-fixing arrangements with contracts totaling $1,800,000 – a cool $500,000 higher than they should have been.

Alert taxpayers saw through the ruse and immediately went to court to halt the theft of public money with a complaint alleging conspiracy and collusion. Governor Olson made an attempt to block the inquiry by

A porch at the Athletic Club in Minneapolis.
Photo courtesy of the Hennepin County Library.

conducting an independent investigation. In the meantime, Attorney General Harry W. Benson ruled that the work should continue so that struggling employees would continue to be paid. At the time the ruling was made, the contractors offered to accept a discount of 20 percent off their contracts – a sure sign they were over-charging the taxpayer. A long and expensive lawsuit followed the accusations of bid-rigging and, in the end, the six contractors were compelled by court action to return $400,000 to the state. When commenting on the case, the Minnesota Supreme Court suggested:

> "It could hardly be expected that the regulations and limitations would result in fair competition among bidders. Limiting the number of bidders and restricting the amount of construction to be let to each during 1932 was scarcely less than an invitation to get favored contractors to get together and do just what it is they allegedly did do – conspire to obtain the work at an exorbitant profit."

State Purchasing Commissioner Carl Erickson was found innocent, having merely followed the Governor's orders.

Steel Bids

On November 31, 1931, four companies turned in bids which had been called for by Commissioner Babcock to provide steel for road construction. Prior to Olson's inauguration, contractors purchased their own steel. Shortly after the bids were received, Olson sent letters to the bidders advising them their bids had been thrown out.

Several days prior, Babcock signed a contract with the Paper Calmenson Company for 10,000 tons of steel. Ironically, the Paper Calmenson Company had not even proffered a bid and the price was estimated by experts as being at least $10,000 higher than the market would bear.

David Paper, president of the company with the winning contract, was rumored to be a close friend of Olson and one of his most active supporters. His relationship with Olson appeared to pay off when yet another bid was let to provide steel for a new state office building. Although T. F. McCormick came in as the low bidder at $27,860 and was advised to draw up a contract by contractor Walter Magee, the sale was awarded to Paper Calmenson Company with a bid of $31,473.

Imported Potatoes

On June 1, 1925, the Minnesota Colony for Epileptics was opened in Cambridge. The first patients were transferred from the Minnesota School for the Feeble Minded and Colony for Epileptics at Faribault. The school ran under the auspices of the Board of Control, comprised of three members appointed by the Governor with the consent of the Senate, with at least one woman as a member. The appointments were for a period of six years. Under the Minnesota Commitment Law, probate courts committed "feebleminded" persons to the guardianship of the State Board of Control, and not the institution.

On, or around June 20, 1931, the Board of Control was in the market for potatoes to feed residents of the Minnesota Colony for Epileptics. In a somewhat surprising move, the Board, rather than purchase potatoes from local dealers who offered to deliver the potatoes sacked and weighed for 80 cents a bushel, instead bought potatoes from 1,500 miles away in Washington state. The Board not only discriminated against local farmers, but wasted taxpayer money on shipping costs which benefited the railroads and those making commissions on the sale of potatoes.

The Minneapolis Alderman Graft Case of 1928

In his book, *Minneapolis in the Twentieth Century; The Growth of an American City*, Iric Nathanson calls Hennepin County Attorney Floyd B. Olson a "crusading reformer" who spearheaded an investigation against Minneapolis City Council members suspected of receiving bribes from businessmen.

In contrast, investigative journalist Walter Liggett accused Olson of trying to hush the rumored bribery of Minneapolis aldermen. The scandal only became public after Louis N. Ritten, a grain dealer and president of the Council, sought immunity and offered to turn state's evidence for accepting a $500 bribe from John Woodward and Werner H. Ruff. The two businessmen were granted a license to open The Stables. Ritten went to the prosecuting attorney and signified his willingness to confess to the City Council's indiscretions. Frank Brunskill, former chief of police of Minneapolis, and then investigator, advised Ritten to hire Archie M. Cary as his attorney. Ritten paid Cary a $5,000 retaining fee, eventually spending $12,000 for his defense.

Several days later Ritten met Olson at the Minneapolis Athletic Club. By this time Ruff and Woodward had provided the county attorney with information about the bribery. Nevertheless, Olson granted Ritten immunity. Within days, Ritten appeared before a grand jury and confessed, implicating at least half a dozen of his fellow council members.

Ritten disappeared from Minneapolis shortly after testifying. Hennepin County Grand Jury Foreman Dean E. E. Nicholson, a University of Minnesota faculty member, was convinced that Ritten had not been completely forthcoming. Nicholson, along with two reporters from the Minneapolis Journal, traced Ritten to the Pacific Coast and convinced him to return to Minneapolis to make a complete confession.
During the trip home, the group's luggage was stolen and Ritten's room was searched by a detective. Papers relating to an investigation into

racketeering within the dry cleaning and dyeing industries in the Twin Cities were stolen by an agent shadowing the group.

Louis N. Ritten, Minneapolis Alderman.
Photo courtesy of the Hennepin County Library.

Upon his return to the Twin Cities, and fearing for his life, Ritten registered at the Commodore Hotel in St. Paul under the name C.W. Farnsworth. He continued his interview with the reporters. The group was badly shaken when five plainclothes policemen barreled through a hotel door with side arms drawn in response to a phone call reporting strange behavior.

In his affidavit, Ritten declared:

> I want to reveal everything to clear my conscience of these regrettable affairs. At the same time I wish to call the attention of the grand jury to the long standing practice of wealthy businessmen and firms of contributing to the corruption of the municipal and other public officials. The City Council of Minneapolis has been subjected to graft for a long time; it has been a common practice for businessmen wanting assistance or business to approach aldermen with offers of money. . . . Aldermen are not alone responsible for the present situation in Minneapolis. Some of the blame should be placed on the shoulders of these business firms who solicit business by holding out a roll of bills to city officials.

According to journalist Liggett, County Attorney Olson was furious. Olson went directly to the district court and had Nicholson removed as foreman of the grand jury with the pretext that he had "concealed evidence."

Ritten's testimony about bribes paid to Minneapolis council members totaled sixty typewritten pages and named a variety of Minneapolis businessmen and dealers for outside equipment firms. Thirty-three indictments were returned and four councilmen and three minor neighborhood politicians were committed to Stillwater State Prison. Liggett pointed out that, with the exception of James E. Fox, broker for a group of oil companies which obtained lucrative contracts through bribery, not one other wealthy businessman spent a single day in prison. Nor were they ever indicted.

Fox was interviewed by local newspaper reporters and threatened to "blow the lid off of city hall" with inside information, but didn't carry through on his threat. His case was settled with a guilty plea – under the consent of Prosecuting Attorney Olson. A demand for Fox to pay a $750 fine resulted, which made up only a fraction of the $10,000 fine or ten-year conviction he could have received for his crime. Olson explained his leniency was due to an implied consent by Fox to help the city recover large sums of money lost through the granting of contracts to oil companies who bribed officials for favorable rates. Fox vanished shortly after his trial with no records supporting the notion that Minneapolis ever recovered any of its losses with his assistance.

Likewise, in the Eighth Ward graft trials, Street Commissioner Maurice Ring, appointed by Alderman W. Harry Rendell and working under Rendell's orders, sold city property and pocketed the proceeds. He was also accused of forging names on public payrolls, defrauding the city of thousands of dollars. Ring was tried twice in trials which were, according to gossip in Hennepin County, poorly prosecuted, leaving the juries undecided. Despite also being under indictment, Alderman Rendell was allowed to appear as a character witness for Ring. And although Ring's testimony brought to light the existence of a widespread conspiracy, no one was ever convicted of a crime. Ring died before his third trial began.

After the trials and sentencing were over, Olson took credit for the investigation and its resulting convictions, a storyline local newspapers generously proffered to the public. With the newspapers' assistance, Olson burnished his reputation as an intrepid prosecutor and exceptional candidate for governor.

Rental Property Rates

The Olson administration was accused of showing favoritism to a variety of businesses including rental properties owned by colorful businessman Charles Ward, president of Brown & Bigelow Printing. A new seven-story state office building for public officials was completed on November 15, 1932, at a cost of $1,485,000 with the expectation that it would fulfill their needs for years to come. Yet, the Olson administration was paying $84,596 annually for outside office space while the Old State Capital on Wabasha and Tenth Streets in St. Paul sat boarded and empty.

State Treasurer Julius A. Schmahl drew up a schedule of rent paid in 1933, which included the cost of rent for state agencies. Schmahl did not include additional rental costs for the Grain Inspection Department. Rentals were estimated by experts to be excessive, particularly when conditions of the buildings were taken into consideration. The inflated rents continued to be paid to Ward

Oppenheimer Seeks a Cellmate for Bigelow

William Oppenheimer (circa 1913)
Photo Courtesy of Oppenheimer, Wolff & Donnelly Archives

Charlie Ward came to Minnesota upon the suggestion of prominent Twin Cities businessman Hubert Huse Bigelow. The invitation was extended during the time the two were in Leavenworth Prison together. Bigelow was serving an unexpectedly severe sentence for tax evasion, the result of the first such suit brought by the United States Government after the implementation of the Income Tax Law. Bigelow opposed the new tax which took effect when the Sixteenth Amendment was ratified on February 13, 1913. He refused to pay income taxes. Bigelow served as chief executive officer of Brown & Bigelow, a printing company co-founded with Hiram Brown in 1896 in St. Paul. Brown was never active in running the company and died in 1905.

The tax case was prosecuted in the Old Federal Courts building in 1924 with Bigelow represented by attorney Will Oppenheimer. Stan D. Donnelly represented Brown & Bigelow's treasurer. Donnelly's client was acquitted, but Bigelow was sentenced to three years in Leavenworth.

Oppenheimer and Donnelly were impressed with one another's skills as attorneys and Oppenheimer, who had a reputation for being one of the first business-minded lawyers in St. Paul, badly wanted Donnelly to join his firm. Donnelly, a prominent and influential member of the Irish community, initially refused Oppenheimer's offer. But, in 1925, he accepted full partnership with the agreement that he could vacation during the entire month of July at his family's Bemidji home and also take two weeks off to play golf. With Donnelly now on board, the firm was ranked the second largest law practice in St Paul. When word spread about the new vacation policies, jobs at the firm became coveted positions.

Oppenheimer took good care of his employees. He also gave to the community, investing his talent and time in pro bono work. It should have come as no surprise when, in 1927, Oppenheimer was awarded the title "Rebuilder of St. Paul." His generous spirit was essential to the city in the early part of the century, because St. Paul was in trouble. The city was infested with gangsters who knew they would be given safe haven in St. Paul through Police Chief John O'Connor's layover agreement. For a few bucks, criminals could seek asylum in the city as long as they promised not to commit crimes within city limits.

In 1929, newspaper editor Howard Kahn began raging against the O'Connor machine in the St. Paul Daily News. Oppenheimer supported him, accompanying Kahn to a meeting with St. Paul Mayor William Mahoney who resented being put in the spotlight. Mahoney demanded proof from Kahn that the O'Connor system existed. According to a newspaper article by Lawrence Platt, Oppenheimer told the mayor that his client would cooperate in a properly constituted judicial process, but not a one-sided star chamber proceeding which grossly violated standards of due process. This so incensed the mayor that he ordered O'Connor to arrest Kahn on the spot. O'Connor, apparently swayed by Oppenheimer's rhetoric, declined. Hearings were set, but somehow the mayor's office always delayed them until finally they dwindled away.

The O'Connor system inevitably affected Minneapolis, St. Paul's twin city across the Mississippi River. According to an article published in the *Aberdeen American* on December 15, 1916, Minneapolis Chief of Police Oscar Martinson was ordered to shoot to kill in response to a rash of crimes riddling the city. Mayor Wallace G. Nye issued orders to plainclothes police officers to feel free to stop crimes with gunfire. The influx of criminal activity was blamed on a lack of harmony between the St. Paul and Minneapolis police forces.

"Some of the criminals, of course, live here," said Mayor Nye, "but the ones who have caused us so much trouble of late are working out of St. Paul, I believe."

In response, St. Paul Police Chief O'Connor said that the Minneapolis police were welcome to make arrests in his city, whether working with the assistance of local police or by themselves.

Oppenheimer looked after his clients with the same dedication directed toward his employees and community. When Bigelow walked into prison with an aristocratic air, Oppenheimer took steps to find a prisoner who could afford Bigelow the most protection. That prisoner turned out to be Charles Ward, a man who had spent a great deal of his life in the presence of organized crime and who had once fought with the Mexican revolutionary Poncho Villa. The two became cellmates.

Bigelow was impressed with his cellmate and found Ward to be "made of good clay," eventually offering him employment with Brown & Bigelow when he finished his prison sentence.

Elizabeth Johanneck

A Word About Charlie Ward

Charlie Ward was born in Seattle to a school teacher and his wife, who struggled to make ends meet. The couple divorced when Ward was fourteen; his mother remarried. Ward took odd jobs selling newspapers, shining shoes and working in a saloon. He ran away from home at seventeen and learned survival tips from other homeless people. Twice he stowed away on ships crossing the Pacific. He made his way to Nome, Alaska, where he once again worked odd jobs and tried his luck at mining gold. The effort paid off and he earned a little money, then doubled it by gambling.

Ward eventually landed in Mexico, serving under Poncho Villa during the revolution as soldiers drove wealthy landowners off land stolen by Conquistadors for Spain. He obtained permission from Villa to collect cattle hides left behind by soldiers who'd slaughtered the animals for food. Ward amassed a small fortune of $70,000. He left the army and returned to the United States where his lavish lifestyle in El Paso, Texas, drew the attention of federal narcotics agents who suspected his money was derived from the drug-smuggling trade.

Ward burned through his savings and eventually drifted to Denver where the authorities were alerted to his presence. Cocaine and morphine were discovered among his belongings – "planted," Ward contended. The 34-year-old was sentenced to Leavenworth. There he met 53-year-old Bigelow and helped make the older man's prison stay bearable. Bigelow was freed after eight months and invited Ward to come to St. Paul upon his release. He would have a job waiting for Ward.

Bigelow met Ward's train and served him lunch in his own home. Ward moved into a rooming house near the printing plant and set to work distinguishing himself as a model employee. In six years he worked his way up from general laborer to general manager. Ward had a keen mind, making Brown & Bigelow a world-class operation. He put the sales force on an incentive pay plan, backed unionization, and broadened the product line to include playing cards, pens, pencils and cigarette lighters. But his most significant accomplishment was securing the artwork of Norman Rockwell, Max Parrish and Rolf Armstrong for calendars. Ward employed fellow prison hands, including a former warden from Leavenworth who had bossed him around. The warden became chief of maintenance for Brown & Bigelow's half-dozen plants.

Ward was rightly rewarded for his good work. But in a suspicious turn of events, eight months after Ward was promoted to vice president, the bodies of Bigelow, aged 63, and Mrs. Ralph Mather, 39, were found in Bass Lake, 20 miles north of Ely. The two disappeared during a fateful hunting trip with a party that included Ralph Mathers and Ward. Mathers and Ward returned safely, but their guide, Howard Schaeffer, disappeared altogether. Ward personally headed up the search party which located the bodies. The executors of Bigelow's estate, Will Oppenheimer and the president of the First National Bank of St. Paul, Richard Lilly, selected Ward to head up Brown & Bigelow.

A reporter from *Time* magazine interviewed Ward in October 1933 for his reaction to the news that Bigelow had drowned. At the time of the interview, Ward had just inherited $1,000,000 from Bigelow's estate. His disposition was reported as being jovial, with Ward going so far as to give the reporter a gold cigarette lighter as a souvenir.

Years later, in July 1947, The *Los Angeles Examiner* announced that Ward was under investigation by the Federal Bureau of Investigation after the discovery of information on two loan payments totaling $100,000 were found among Bugsy Siegel's belongings. The papers were found during the FBI's investigation of "Murder Incorporated," the enforcement arm of the American Mafia and Jewish Mafia in the 1930s and 40s. The first letter bore the signature of Charles Ward and was dated October 14, 1937, written on Brown & Bigelow stationery shortly after Siegel became the Murder Incorporated West Coast representative. The letter read:

> "Dear Ben: Enclosed find two Liberty Bonds for $20,000. Sorry I couldn't make it $25,000, but as you know I am short on cash on account of my stock deals. Am lucky to have enough to eat on. Hope that will help."

The second letter was dated December 6, 1937, on Midway National Bank, St. Paul stationery. This letter was signed by A.L. Ritt and read:

"Dear Mr. Siegel: At the request of Mr. Charles Ward we are enclosing our draft No. 7128 in the amount of $80,000 drawn on the Guarantee Trust Company of New York, payable to yourself. Will you kindly acknowledge receipt and forward same in the enclosed envelope."

Ward explained to the FBI that the payments were for a loan he had received from Siegel. When Siegel was asked if he had been in St. Paul at about the time of Bigelow's death, he denied it and the line of questioning was dropped.

In his book *John Dillinger Slept Here*, Paul MacCabee details the murder of bootlegger Abe Wagner, who was hiding out in St. Paul, at the hands of George Young and Joseph Schaefer, two hit men from Murder Incorporated. Young and Schaefer were captured and convicted of murder on November 11, 1932, and were sentenced to life at hard labor in Stillwater State Prison. The two enjoyed special privileges in the prison, each receiving a $50 weekly stipend which could be used to bribe prison officials.

Fellow prisoner Leonard Hankins, in whom they later confided, informed the FBI that Charlie Ward had been the pair's guardian angel.

1940 – 1950s

Mayor Marvin Kline.
Photo courtesy of the Hennepin County Library.

When future United States Vice President Hubert H. Humphrey ran for mayor of Minneapolis, promising to clean house and rid the city of corruption, the process of winning the office and replacing Mayor Marvin L. Kline was a good first step. With close ties to gangster Davie Berman, Kline was part of the problem. Kline's influence helped make outsider Berman a serious rival to local organized crime figure Kid Cann.

Humphrey began his political career by running for mayor of Minneapolis at the age of 34. He won the election and served from 1945 – 1949. Humphrey stated his reason for running, identifying the problem of organized crime:

" I am motivated to file for mayor because I am convinced that the people of Minneapolis need to be told what is going on in their city. They need to know that Mayor Kline is supported by the racketeering elements in this community and that he does their bidding by permitting illegitimate rackets to operate without restraint.

It is common knowledge among persons who are familiar with what goes on in this city that two groups known as the "syndicate" and the "combination," tell Mayor Kline what he can and what he can't do.

The people of Minneapolis need to be told the facts about the underworld operations in this city. They need to be told about the illicit connections that now exist between the mayor's office and the underworld. I intend to tell the public these facts.

It is time that the good people of this community – good, law-abiding, God fearing people – remove from control of our government the vicious group of racketeers who now dictate.

The public must be informed of the manner in which our police department affords protection to the illegitimate racketeers. I have talked with many patrolmen who tell me they are forced to take "pay-off" money and keep their mouths shut or else be assigned to undesirable beats.

The half-hearted manner in which the police department went about trying to find the murderer of Arthur Kasherman is evidence of the link between the mayor's office and the underworld.

White slavery has been rampant in Minneapolis and it took the federal government to begin a cleanup of the city.

There are hundreds of slot machines operating in Minneapolis for which the owners pay federal licenses, but which the police department can't find.

This situation must be cleaned up, if we are to have a healthy city. Juvenile delinquency has been sharply on the increase, and the mayor has done nothing to stop its growth. It is time that the people of Minneapolis wake up. I intend to tell them the facts."

Humphrey's platform of cleaning up the city was the perfect counterpoint to Mayor Kline's crooked administration. Although Kline was a Republican, the business community showed surprisingly little support for him and Labor did not trust him. He avoided enforcing liquor and gambling laws and it was common knowledge that City Hall and the police department were under the influence of racketeers.

Hubert Humphrey.
Photo courtesy of the Hennepin County Library.

J. Bradshaw Mintener, general counsel for Pillsbury Flour Mills, was Humphrey's biggest supporter in the business industry. When confronted with the concerns of a fellow Republican candidate, Mintener asked if he preferred a gangster in power, or a decent administration.

Humphrey won the 1945 mayoral election handily with 61 percent of the vote, including Kline's home ward. Humphrey had received a mandate from Minneapolis to clean up the city and his first move was to cleanse the police department. He considered a functional police department a vital ingredient of community health.

In his battle against corruption, Humphrey set two goals. One was to increase the size of the police force, enabling the department to concentrate on lowering violent crime. The other was to find a means of reducing juvenile delinquency.

He selected FBI-trained Edwin Ryan, a friend and former neighbor, to head the department's internal security division. It was a difficult confirmation, opposed by city labor unions concerned about Ryan's FBI background making unions a target.

Ryan became an effective and efficient anti-corruption leader. He began his tenure by forcing the resignations of police officers with a history of being on the take. He went after illegal gambling establishments hiding throughout Minneapolis, literally destroying roulette wheels with sledgehammers.

In the meantime, Humphrey instructed a grand jury to review the city's liquor licenses, keeping an eye out for the issuance of multiple licenses to corrupt individuals in order to break the hold of organized crime over the liquor industry. The grand jury delivered a report charging gross negligence in the issuance of licenses and recommended the city create a separate licensing bureau. Minneapolis experienced some improvement in the visible vice operations, but racketeers Kid Cann and Tommy Banks continued to have a stranglehold.

A social worker and four additional policemen were added to the juvenile division of the police force and Ryan created a civilian juvenile-welfare commission to oversee youth-related agencies. In 1946, an executive order replaced the old chain of command in which every division of the Minneapolis police force reported directly to the chief. This change and the implementation of detailed record keeping created more transparency within the department.

The changes in law enforcement paid off with fewer robberies, aggravated assaults and murders in the last two years of Humphrey's term. Violence and vice, though, endured.

Mayor Kline Shakes Down Sister Kenny

Sister Elizabeth Kenney.
Photo courtesy of the Hennepin County Library.

As for Marvin L. Kline, the former mayor joined the private workforce in Minneapolis. Kline was a strong supporter of Sister Elizabeth Kenny, a brilliant bush nurse from New South Wales. Kenny, using common sense, developed an innovative way to treat polio through movement and the use of moist hot packs applied to stiff muscles rather than through immobilization, the accepted treatment at the time. However, she had to battle the American Medical Association to take her work seriously. Kline championed the creation of a clinic for Sister Kenny in Minneapolis.

The Sister Kenny Foundation was established in 1943. Three years later, upon his retirement as mayor, Kline accepted a position as the Foundation's executive director. He began his tenure with a salary of $12,500, eventually raising it to $48,000. Additionally, Kline's compensation through special funds and pension plans totaled $773,013, a bundle which didn't include the car he charged to the Foundation and his all-expense paid trips to foreign countries.

Public relations counsel Fred Fadell was paid an annual salary of $24,700 by Sister Kenny. In 1951 Kline and Fadell set up the Special Events Committee which operated outside of Sister Kenny. As directors of the committee, Kline and Fadell conspired to award a non-competitive contract to the Koolish Companies of Chicago. From 1952 to 1959, Empire Industries, a fundraising company working with Koolish, was selected to raise funds for the Sister Kenny Foundation. The company was extremely successful, soliciting nearly $20,000,000 for the Foundation. Of that bounty, only $8,000,000 found its way to Sister Kenny. Empire kept $11,500,000 to cover its expenses and commissions.

In the contract, Koolish was to refund Sister Kenny for any differences between the actual cost of fundraiser mailings and the amount paid by Sister Kenny. Kline and Fadell provided the Koolish Companies with a list of Foundation contributors. Those names were then given to LeMarge Mailing Company, Inc., a firm owned by Koolish.

Kline and Fadell allowed the Koolish Company to charge the Foundation $25 per thousand names to unnecessarily key-punch them onto computer cards for a new IBM system. Had they stayed with the system used in previous years using typewriters, the cost would have been $8.80 per thousand and would have been sufficient for the Foundation's purpose.

In providing Sister Kenny with a "special donors" list, Koolish actually sold the Foundation's own donor list—millions of names Sister Kenny had collected from 1952-1959—back to the Foundation at a cost of $20 per thousand.

Fadell's good work didn't go unnoticed and he was shown appreciation by Empire Industries in a payoff of $359,200. Fadell, in turn, showed

Kline appreciation by splitting the bonus with him and throwing in a piano to boot.

The scam was investigated by another future United States Vice President, then acting Minnesota Attorney General Walter F. Mondale, who blew the whistle on Kline. In the end, Kline and Fadell, along with mail solicitors Abraham L. Koolish, David F. Koolish, John B. Carnell, Philip G. Rettig and J. George Zimmerman of Chicago were indicted by a grand jury and charged with sixteen counts of mail fraud. Kline was sentenced to five years in prison and ordered to pay $17,000. Fadell was sentenced to a term of imprisonment for a period of one year and one day upon a guilty plea.

Sister Kenny with Mayor Marvin Kline.
Photo courtesy of the Hennepin County Library.

CHAPTER 4
PORNOGRAPHY

Odd Gifts from Mr. X

After all of this time, Mr. X finally remembered to bring the Christmas gifts he promised when we met at the pizza place to review my book. There, in a red and green patterned gift bag, were a hollowed out hand grenade, which frightened me, and a darling brass Thompson machine gun cigarette lighter about nine inches long.

The items had a feeling about them, almost like the whisper of a memory – perhaps from an old gangster movie I had seen as a child. As I ran my fingers along the barrel of the machine gun, I couldn't help thinking about investigative journalist Walter Liggett, gunned down in front of his wife and little girl.

In spite of the danger of being a criminal, there is something a little thrilling about it all. I swear I was a gangster's girl in another lifetime.

Minneapolis' Porn Industry

The Midwest. It sounds like such a wholesome place. But don't be fooled. The Midwest has been touched by every type of vice, including pornography and obscene literature.

One of the first obscene magazines to hit the territory of Minnesota was the innocuously named tabloid, *National Police Gazette*, founded in New York in 1845. It became a source of anxiety for mothers and preachers, but a great delight for many men.

Former law clerk George Wilkes and lawyer Enoch E. Camp, along with editor Richard Kyle Fox, created the publication which featured stories of murder, rape, seduction and other nefarious crimes. The stories were illustrated with images of scantily clad strippers, burlesque dancers, women in quasi-lesbian poses and prostitutes. The magazine also included sports information, particularly boxing.

Within several months of debuting, the publication had 15,000 subscribers and is credited with being the inspiration for magazines like *Sports Illustrated, Playboy,* and the *National Enquirer.* The *National Police Gazette* carried provocative stories from every state, including Minnesota.

When the railroad barons established a transportation hub in Minneapolis for shipping goods and people, they also started a base for the importation of the darker things in life. Questionable literature was shipped to the city by the carful. Even at that, it took a while before the ethical decline became evident. When that happened, the *National Police Gazette* would be there to report it.

On January 10, 1856, two years before Minnesota became a state, Minnesota Territorial Governor Willis Arnold Gorman praised Minnesota before the House of Representatives for its honorable ways. Expounding upon the blessings granted to the territory by the Almighty, he stated:

> "The soil has yielded abundant crops, commerce and the mechanic arts have flourished, and morality and education have kept pace with other elements of greatness and success"

But, in truthfulness, Minnesota was struggling with its morality. Meanwhile, back East, in 1873, politician Anthony Comstock created the *Society for the Suppression of Vice* of New York City to supervise the decency of the public. Later that same year, he convinced Congress to pass the Comstock Law, which made it illegal to transport and deliver obscene, lewd or lascivious material. This included any documents pertaining to birth control or the spread of sexually transmitted diseases.

In 1885, under the direction of Comstock, a postal agent traveled to Minnesota, prowling for vice and violators selling the *National Police Gazette* and similar publications. He intended to sue them. Interviewed by the *Duluth News-Tribune*, the agent was asked how he spotted these men. He replied that he always visited barbershops first for a shave, slyly perusing the literature. Then he would stay in lower-rate hotels and survey their inventory of books and magazines. Lastly, the agent checked out every saloon in town looking for lewd, vulgar, or obscene pictures and publications.

The investigator then singled out the worst violator in town for prosecution, calling on other offenders to choose either prosecution or settlement. Those who chose not to settle were then "prosecuted in a lump."

When the unnamed man was asked which city was the vilest, he credited Duluth – by a big majority.

From these activities, George Bernard Shaw, playwright and founder of the London School of Economics coined the word "Comstockery," suggesting that the United States looked like a joke to the rest of the civilized world with its Victorian ways. In return, Comstock called Shaw "an Irish smut dealer."

Jim Jam Jems

In 1912, a new magazine, *Jim Jam Jems*, "Official Magazine of the Bar Flies of America," hit the streets of Minneapolis. Published in Bismarck, North Dakota, the magazine was used by Sam Clark as a vehicle to expose corruption of the Federal Reserve, unjust wars, and even addressed infant mortality through humor, satire, sensationalism, and social and political commentary.

Each month the magazine fired a "volley of truth" about the ills of the nation under the name Jim Jam Junior.

The federal government tried to close the magazine down and denied it the right to be transported across state lines. The effort backfired. Before long *Jim Jam Jems* had become the most popular magazine in the nation.

On April 4, 1912, six Minneapolis men were indicted for selling *Jim Jam Jems* and for the distribution of obscene literature. On December 10, 1912, a Minneapolis grand jury acquitted them, declaring *Jim Jam Jems* "real literature" and going so far as to suggest that the general public should be reading it. "We don't see anything in any of the numbers that ought to be classified as obscene."

Reverend, Go Lightly

With United States postal inspectors acting as censors for the public, many types of literature could be classified as obscene based on one man's understanding or the government's quest for control of information and nonconformist opinions

For a while in the early 1900s, Minneapolis was home to a colorful writer, the Rev. Giulian L. Morrill. As a pastor, he was once advised by an associate that Minneapolis Baptist Church officials were getting uneasy about his nontraditional hosting of musicians, hula dancers, slide shows and drummers at his services. The associate suggested that Morrill had better "go lightly." That nickname stuck with Morrill until he left his church in 1903 to found the unorthodox People's Church in Minneapolis.

In 1917, en route to Ecuador, Morrill was arrested in New Orleans on charges issued by a federal grand jury. He was accused of sending obscenity through the mail. The accusation was based on a graphic description of a hanging published in his book, *The Devil in Mexico*. He was brought back to Minneapolis and, after several postponements, the government dropped the case.

Six years later, in 1923, a Hennepin County grand jury brought charges against the reverend, this time in connection with an advertisement placed in a local newspaper. This case, too, was eventually dismissed.

Morrill was as colorful in death as he was in life. In 1928, he had the distinction of giving the eulogy at his own funeral, having recorded his thoughts on a wax record months earlier. The recording was played near his casket.

Minneapolis' Femme Fatale

Annette Fawcett publisher of *The Eye Opener*.
Photo courtesy of the Hennepin County Library.

With the documented history of organized crime dominated by the bad behavior of men, it is often difficult to learn about the women who were mixed up with them. But in Minneapolis, one well-known femme fatale, Antoinette (Annette) Fischer Fawcett, *the "Henna Haired Hurricane of Laughter and Joy,"* made the papers. She was the second wife of Captain Billy Fawcett, publishing magnate and owner of Breezy Point Lodge near Brainerd.

Fawcett started his publishing empire with a naughty little rag, *Whiz Bang*, originally created in the 1920s for WW I soldiers recovering in the VA hospital. However, the rag grew in popularity among the general public with Annette Fawcett credited for "putting the sizzle" in *Whiz Bang*.

The marriage didn't last, possibly due to an alleged affair with Governor Floyd B. Olson, mentioned in Marda Liggett Woodbury's book, *Stopping the Presses*. Mrs. Fawcett moved into room 1013 in the Radisson Hotel where she entertained every celebrity and high-class criminal visiting the city. The Fawcetts' divorce was extremely acrimonious and Mrs. Fawcett's indiscretions are well-documented. In his testimony to the court, Captain Billy accused her of making much of herself, belittling him and putting him down as a "chore boy." He went on to declare that she failed to show him respect and loyalty and complained she used uncomplimentary terms when speaking of him to other people. She appeared nice to his face, then berated him behind his back.

Anne Roberts, a waitress at Breezy Point and personal maid for Mrs. Fawcett, testified that her employer spent large amounts of money throwing parties without her husband's knowledge. The bookkeeper at the resort, Charles W. Henderson, admitted Mrs. Fawcett had charge accounts all over the world. Other employees attested to her alcohol use and uncontrollable temper.

Mrs. Fawcett was granted $60,000 in the divorce settlement and, in 1932, used the money to purchase a competing magazine, *Eye Opener,* from her brother-in-law, Harvey Fawcett. It was a pocket-sized piece of literature packed with naughty limericks and stories about lost virginity. Harvey Fawcett originally purchased the rights to the magazine in 1922 after founder Robert Chamber Edwards, from near Calgary, Alberta, died. Harvey Fawcett began an American version, but continued printing the Canadian edition, bringing the magazine's files to Minneapolis.

The new publisher was a poor manager whose business decisions were often made while under the influence of alcohol. The magazine was failing when Annette Fawcett purchased the periodical and hired men who could run it profitably. But she spent the profit as quickly as it was made. *Eye Openers'* employees met with Annette Fawcett and advised her that if she did not turn the day-to-day operations over to them, the business would go bankrupt. She could still remain editor, but would need to keep her fingers out of the till. She agreed to the business arrangement, and also to adding photos of nude women.

U.S. Commissioner Howard S. Abbott caught whiff of the impropriety and charged Fawcett and three others with sending obscene matter through the mail, specifically for shipping porn over the state line. The offending magazine was the *"Eye Opener's Annual Red Pepper, Sixth Edition"* and *"Old Nick's Annual TNT."* The complaint was sworn to by H. E. Alford, Washington Post Office Inspector. Warrants were issued for Fawcett, Charles F. Zinn, Phil Rolfson and Rose Fjelde, with the defendant company listed as Bob Edwards Publishing Company.

The magazine eventually went bankrupt. Fawcett had additional scrapes with the law for speeding and shoplifting.

Hub of Indecency

National newspapers identified Minneapolis as a hub for pornography in 1944, after postal inspectors and the FBI discovered evidence that Minneapolis was the center of nationwide trafficking. Raids uncovered more than 10,000 books of obscene literature, along with thousands of lewd photographs. The raid in 1944, on a hotel room, resulted in the arrests of eight individuals, three of them women.

Local resident Ferris Alexander, who earned the nickname "Patriarch of Porn," began his career with his brother, Edward, in a newsstand at South Fourth Street and East Hennepin Avenue in Minneapolis. The business started innocently enough with several racy photos under the counter. But the photos didn't stay there for long. It seems the men of Minneapolis had an appetite for erotica.

The Alexanders, who would eventually be known to organized crime members as the Lebanese Alexander Brothers, discovered that the images of naked women – tasteful by today's standards – were a pot of gold. The brothers took advantage of the demand for porn by stocking *Sunshine Health*, a magazine intended for nudists.

Headquarters of AB Enterprises, the Alexanders' business, eventually relocated to Lake Street and Third Avenue. The Lebanese Alexander Brothers then expanded, buying up commercial property to house adult bookstores. They eventually populated Minneapolis with movie theaters showing professionally produced X-rated films from New York. This was the heyday of artistic pornography. The quality of films quickly declined at the advent of hand-held video equipment. Soon anyone could produce porn.

The Alexanders began purchasing their films from California. The demand grew for more diverse types of pornography—such as gay and lesbian—with the explosion of low-quality films. The brothers continued purchasing commercial property, opening additional X-rated theaters, bookstores and houses of prostitution. They also opened tawdry shops lined with booths shielded by curtains that allowed an individual to slip quarters into a slot and watch a few minutes of grainy, silent pornography on a small screen.

In the 1960s they expanded into the movie industry, occupying theaters on Lake Street, an area in economic and moral decline. People stood in a line that wound around the block in 1969 to watch Alexander's flagship X-rated movie, *I am Curious Yellow*, at the Rialto Theater, 735 East Lake Street.

The Alexanders' success was soon noticed by the New York based Genovese crime family and a relationship was established between them. The family had so much faith in Ferris Alexander's abilities, that, in 1981, he was sent to Kansas City to take over for crime boss Giuseppe Nicoli "Nick" Civella. The crime leader was serving a prison sentence for conspiring to bribe a Fort Worth prison warden into transferring his nephew from a federal prison in Texarkana, Texas, to the Fort Worth facility.

Ironically, Civella shared a cell in Leavenworth with Minneapolis' former Baldy and organized crime figure Deuce Casper, who was considered tough enough to protect Civella from other prisoners.

President's Commission on Obscenity and Pornography

In 1968, President Lyndon Johnson created the President's Commission on Obscenity and Pornography, also known as the *Lockhart Report*. Serving as chairman of the commission was William Lockhart, dean of the University of Minnesota Law School, who, the *Associated Press* reported, supported the findings of the commission. Lockhart agreed there should be no restrictions on the sale of pornography to adults and that it was not the government's role to impose moral standards on its citizens. He addressed 400 lawyers at a meeting of the Hennepin County Bar Association, advising them that the report's findings indicated explicit sexual material was not harmful to adults. The report also supported the creation of massive sex education programs. Of the eighteen commission members, only two were women.

On October 24, 1970, President Richard M. Nixon responded to the findings of the committee, stating:

> "SEVERAL weeks ago, the National Commission on Obscenity and Pornography-appointed in a previous administration-presented its findings."
>
> "I have evaluated that report and categorically reject its morally bankrupt conclusions and major recommendations."
>
> "So long as I am in the White House, there will be no relaxation of the national effort to control and eliminate smut from our national life . . ."

In 1973, Minneapolis Police Sgt. Jon Prentice, head of the morals squad, expressed his frustration at being unable to close down a showing of the movie *Deep Throat*, considered at the time the most hard-core example of pornography of the decade. He concluded the main problem to be that the general public simply did not consider pornography a serious problem. Law enforcement in New York City was able to cease showing of the film through a criminal court ruling. But the Midwestern cities held out.

Organized Crime and Minneapolis Porn

The 1986 Attorney General's Commission on Pornography, also known as the *Meese Report*, tied Ferris Alexander of the Minneapolis pornographer, Lebanese Alexander Brothers, to the Genovese crime family. According to the report:

> ... Also, a known pornography distributor in Minneapolis, Minnesota, Ferris Alexander was stopped in Los Angeles, California, in the company of William Bittner, also known as William Haimowitz on February 11, 1974. On May 15, 1975, a truckload of pornographic materials was hijacked in St. Paul, Minnesota. The owner of the truck and person reporting the crime was Michael Kaplins of 2014 Westchester, Baltimore, Maryland. At this time, Mr. Kaplins stated that the shipment was being shipped from Bon Jay Sales, 6601 Moravia Park Drive, Baltimore, Maryland, (formerly 600 Aisquith St., Baltimore, Maryland) to a party named Ferris and gave a phone number which was later traced to Ferris Alexander. On September 8, 1975, several cartons of pornographic booklets being shipped by Emery Air Freight broke open. Emery officials refused to deliver the shipment and notified federal and local authorities. The shipment was found to contain material displaying young children and adults in pornographic activity. The pornographic material was being shipped from Atlantic Distributors, #9 Ford St., Providence, Rhode Island, to a magazine Agency, 419 Hennepin Ave., Minneapolis, Minnesota, which is owned by Ferris Alexander.

In the early 1990s, following a four-month trial, a jury convicted Ferris J. Alexander, Sr., on twenty-four counts of a forty-one count indictment. The counts included conspiracy to defraud the IRS, the sale of obscene magazines and videos, tax evasion, and RICO violations. Under the RICO Act, Alexander forfeited three vehicles, numerous properties and roughly $8,000,000 determined to have been raised through racketeering activities from 1985-1988. The court rejected Alexander's argument that such an extreme forfeiture would violate his First Amendment rights, stating that they were inextricably tied to an enormous racketeering enterprise

The pressure was on to stamp out pornography. In an attempt to take down the Alexander porn empire, Kenneth Starr, who also prosecuted the impeachment trial for President Bill Clinton over his extra-marital affair with Monica Lewinsky, brought a suit against Alexander. Starr alleged that Ferris J. Alexander, Sr., for more than thirty years, provided the citizens of Minneapolis with adult entertainment through the sale of books and magazines, pornographic movies shown in theaters, and movie rentals. In the course of doing business, he set up sham corporations under false names and under the names of his employees.

From 1959 – 1978 he used the name Kenneth LaLonde to conduct business under Kenneth LaLonde Enterprises. Attorney R. J. Milavetz was hired by Alexander in 1969 to incorporate this and other businesses, obtain licenses and open bank accounts. The businesses were reported on LaLonde's individual tax return, thereby evading the need to pay corporate taxes.

According to a court appeal filed March 13, 1991, in the United States Court of Appeals, Eighth Circuit - 943 F.2d 825, Milavetz and Alexander had a falling out and, in 1976, Alexander turned to attorney R. Tigue for assistance. Tigue reportedly witnessed LaLonde's signature as incorporator of two more corporations. Alexander's porn industry was consolidated under these corporations.

Then, on May 1, 1977, the name of L. Wendling, another Alexander employee, was substituted as the front name. Bank accounts were opened and the corporations reported to state and federal agencies with Wendling as the owner. In order to sign corporate tax returns, a rubber stamp of Wendling's signature was used. Wendling filed tax returns listing Alexander's income until he was fired at the end of 1980. His name was then replaced with the name John Thomas.

On December 27, 1984, Korean immigrant and Alexander employee S. Na executed the articles of incorporation for ten different companies as incorporator and first director. To further confuse authorities, six of the companies were given Finnish names and four were formed in a dialect of the Philippines. Na filed tax returns and two of the companies were used to buy real estate and a bookstore. Alexander continued starting and incorporating businesses, opening bank accounts and obtaining licenses, and complying with local regulations via additional borrowed front names.

Alexander used a number of tactics to hide his crimes, including sending Milavetz to an unemployment compensation hearing on behalf of Kenneth LaLonde Enterprises. He also sent LaLonde to sign a license application as the owner for the Flick theater. He appeared before the St. Paul City Council for licensing proceedings. When the council objected to granting the license, Tigue advised them that he represented Alexander and LaLonde. He convinced the council that a license existed between the two parties and subsequently filed a lawsuit in United States District Court against the City of St. Paul and its Council members. LaLonde later testified that he only became aware of the lawsuit after he read about it in the paper and that the signature on the complaint, notarized by Tigue, was a forgery. According to court documents, Alexander and Tigue continued securing licenses in LaLonde's name without his knowledge, after LaLonde's employment with Alexander ended.

The proceeds from Alexander's businesses were brought to him at a central warehouse and then distributed to a variety of banks. Other funds were converted into large denominations, cashier checks, and money orders made payable to a variety of entities. Expenses were paid out of primary accounts. Goods were shipped in from California, repackaged and distributed to his retail outlets. When investigators began looking for evidence against Alexander, they found his sloppy bookkeeping a deterrent to the investigation. Still, they estimated that in 1982 and 1983, he had underreported his income each year by over $1,000,000. When admitting in court that he had used his employees' names for nefarious purposes, Alexander suggested that it was Tigue's idea, a charge that Tigue denied.

Alexander appealed the court's decision, arguing that his past was a "series of scenes of hustling," and not a conspiracy. He further argued that the jury did not apply contemporary community standards, but instead made "impermissible distinctions" based on values of taste, morality, and cultural rejection, resulting in inconsistent or compromised verdicts. He suggested that:

> The rationales advanced for criminalization of sexually explicit materials are fundamentally antithetical to the constitutional guarantees of free speech and privacy, and that statutes criminalizing the distribution of obscenity were inherently overbroad and that the Miller test failed to provide fair notice of prohibited speech and encourages arbitrary enforcement, which rendered the federal obscenity statute void for vagueness and unduly chilling free speech.

The jury rejected his arguments, stating their decision:

> ... Does not violate the First Amendment even though certain materials, books and magazines, that are forfeited, may not be obscene and, in other circumstances, would have constitutional protection as free expression. There was a nexus established between defendant's ill gotten gains from their racketeering activities and the protected materials that were forfeited. The forfeiture did not occur until after defendants were convicted of violating various obscenity statutes and of participating in a racketeering activity, and until after it was established beyond a reasonable doubt that the proceeds from these criminal activities had been used to acquire the arguably protected publications.

Alexander died on January 31, 2003, and is buried at Fort Snelling National Cemetery in Minneapolis.

Set on Fire

There is no question the topic of pornography can arouse a great deal of emotion in those who oppose it or who have been deeply affected by it. A prime example of such passion was exhibited on July 10, 1984, when 23-year-old porn protestor, Ruth L. Christenson, poured gasoline over herself and set herself on fire in Schinder's Bookstore at 628 Hennepin in downtown Minneapolis. She wanted to bring attention to the anti-pornography cause.

Christenson received third degree burns over 65 percent of her body and suffered severe disfigurement. Earlier that week she sent a letter to Minneapolis City Council members advising them that, "sexism has shattered my life." Firecrackers, a BB gun, .22-caliber bullets and anti-pornography fliers fell from her backpack as she burned. Six years after setting herself ablaze, Christenson died.

The event took place as the city council was considering revisions to a tough, controversial ordinance to control pornography. Mayor Don Fraser vetoed the ordinance the previous January for being too broad. Outside the city council meeting three days later, protestors linked arms and chanted in support of the ordinance, which resulted in twenty-five arrests. The council passed a revised ordinance which defined pornography as a violation of women's rights, only to have it vetoed by the mayor, a liberal Democrat.

In August of 1984, high profile attorney Gloria Allred agreed with Minneapolis' decision to consider pornography as a civil rights violation and a form of sex discrimination in an opinion piece entitled *"Civil Rights Ideal Weapon in Smut Battle."* She noted that pornographers and civil libertarians opposed the decision. Allred cited studies concluding that pornography increased attitudes and behaviors of violent and non-violent discrimination by men against women, though men, children, and transsexuals could also be affected.

Technology and Porn

As crime became more sophisticated, investigators struggled to keep pace with the skills required to capture online violators. In 1985, the Minneapolis Police Department sought the assistance of a 15-year-old computer hacker to access an electronic diary housed on the computer of a programmer on three years' probation for mailing obscene materials.

In fifteen minutes the teen bypassed the code that had eluded investigators for months. Police knew the young hacker because he had "accidentally" accessed a local bank's computer system.

Though not paid for his time, the youth was advised he could eventually be called as an expert witness at the suspect's trial. The teenager noted that the suspect was a computer programmer who knew computers, but certainly didn't know much about computer security.

CHAPTER 5
SMUGGLING RINGS

We Meet Again

Mr. X and I arranged to meet at the pizza place again and I drove there directly from work. As I pulled into the driveway, I could see Mr. X looking more mob-like than ever. Now that the weather was cool, he donned a long black coat, somehow blacker than any coat I had ever seen. He wore a white scarf around his neck and his hair was, as always, perfectly slicked back. I caught up with him at the door and he complimented me on my promptness.

He let me choose the booth and I picked one that wouldn't be bombarded by sunlight, which I must consider now that I am at that age where heat is my enemy. Who wants hot flashes in the company of a member of organized crime?

Today Mr. X carried a manila envelope with photos of Twin Cities locations frequented by his gang, the Baldies. He also had a nice shot of organized crime member Dave Berman's home. I reviewed the collection, each location identified by writing on the backs of the images.

Then Mr. X asked if I was wearing a wire. Wait. What? I assured him I wasn't. He didn't know that I am more afraid of law enforcement than of him. I can't decide if I should feel flattered or disappointed in his distrust of me. Hasn't he noticed I have never asked him to elaborate on any of the "opportunities" he has mentioned? The less I know about those things, the better.

While we ate, Mr. X regaled me with stories about the local criminal scene and the time he spent with gangster Deuce Casper near the end of Casper's life. Casper founded the Baldies, who rivaled the greaser Animals back in the 1960s.

When our dinner ended and the sun had set, Mr. X walked me to my new second-hand car and looked it over, I suppose for any sign that I was in cahoots with the police. I left the parking lot and headed home wondering once again if I was doing the right thing. What if this brilliant man turned out to be paranoid? What if he convinced himself I was some kind of snitch?

I went to bed that night with organized crime members swirling in my head. And not in a good way.

Elizabeth Johanneck

Smuggling

The act of smuggling products into, through, and out of Minneapolis went on at a brisk pace, thanks to the excellent transportation hub provided by the railroad system. For a time, wealthy Minneapolis residents considered it almost a sport to smuggle goods through customs without paying duty.

In other cases, smuggling was a deadly serious matter. *The Western Appeal*, a noted African-American newspaper published in St. Paul, carried an extensive article on December 31, 1898, which addressed the topic of smuggling with fascinating observations. The article advised the reader:

> Women are all born smugglers, the treasury officials say, and this feminine weakness is so far recognized as beyond their own control that they are almost never prosecuted. The ablest experts in this line are women, some of whom are well known as such to the government officials, and yet are so skillful as to rarely get caught. The favorite way to smuggle diamonds is to ship them from Paris or London, to Montreal, Canada, charging no duty on them, and then take them secretly across the border into the United States. Diamonds are hidden in the heels of shoes, cakes of soap, the hollow legs of dolls, in corks of bottles and even in cheese. Women have been known to wrap them in tissue the color of their hair and work them into their hairstyles where they go undetected. Watches have been smuggled in hollowed out bibles. Oil cans have been used to smuggle fine French brandy, and one dog was known to wear the skin of a larger dog with lace hidden between the two coats. Opium is hidden in oranges and bananas, and one "hump-back" had contraband stored in the lump on his back.

Coffins were regarded with great suspicion. One family in "deep mourning" borrowed the corpse of a pauper in Europe to bring a large quantity of silks and gloves back from France.

Individuals, promised 25 percent of sales proceeds from the seizure of smuggled goods, were encouraged to identify smugglers. That created a black market for spotters watching for smuggling activity.

Diplomats accredited to the United States could bring anything they wanted, duty-free, through customs. This privilege was often abused, for example, by diplomats who brought large quantities of wine into the country to resell. Sometimes the diplomat would come through customs wearing a suit of clothing sewn in France for a wealthy purchaser in the States. Antiques belonging to a period earlier than the 17th Century were allowed in duty-free, but often contained smuggled goods. Skeletons, of which about 1,500 were imported each year from France at the tail-end of the 1800s, were also duty-free.

Tariffs were put in place to control the flow of products onto the American market and to raise money for the government. In 1883, the tariff on opium, refined for smoking, was raised from $6 to $10 a pound. As a result, imports dropped immediately from 288,000 pounds to less than 40,000 pounds per annum. This did not mean less opium was being imported into the country but, rather, more was being smuggled.
In 1889, the tariff was raised again, this time to $12 per pound, putting an additional $2 per pound into the smuggler's pocket. Recognizing no benefit in raising the duty, it was once again lowered to $6. As a result, Uncle Sam earned a bigger share.

Immense capital had been employed in the business of bringing opium into the United States from the British possessions, just as it would be invested in smuggling liquor into the United States during Prohibition.

Drugs

In addition to the illegal flow of liquor from Canada, narcotics were also being smuggled into Minnesota. An extensive smuggling band was discovered in December of 1888, after A. O. Neilson, alias J. M. Leonard, was arrested in Denver. Officials seized 800 pounds of opium along with expensive Chinese silks destined for merchants in the Twin Cities. The smugglers dropped contraband at various destinations along the Canadian Pacific Railroad on the eastern border of the state.

A copy of a waybill from the St. Paul, Minneapolis and Manitoba Railroad was discovered by U.S. Treasury Department Special Agent Mark Harding. Neilson's trunk was searched in his hotel room and found to contain 147 packets of prepared opium weighing 78 pounds. Nielson was jailed in St. Paul.

Railroads like the Northern Pacific were often used for smuggling.
Photo courtesy of the Hennepin County Library.

On September 29, 1911, the *Duluth Tribune* reported the arrest of Chinaman Chow How in Minneapolis for smuggling opium across the Canadian border. Porters and other railway employees were suspected of assisting the smuggling ring.

In the autumn of 1922, a 23-year-old woman was arrested by federal narcotics agents when she boarded a train in Duluth with $3,000 worth of opium in her purse. Margaret Fischer, who lived in a hotel at 223 Cedar

Avenue in Minneapolis, reportedly belonged to an opium smuggling ring with branches in New York City, Buffalo and the Twin Cities.
Duluth police told reporters: "We have been on the trail of one of the cleverest woman smugglers in the United States." She carried the drug in small tin boxes referred to by drug addicts as toys. The tins were often used to pack small quantities of smoking opium parcels suitable for retail sales.

About a decade later, Volume 4 of the 1931 *National Commission on Law Observance and Enforcement Report* described the effort to control the delivery of narcotics into the state. Most of the drugs arrived in Minnesota from New York, Chicago, Kansas City and Canada. The report mentioned two cases of smuggling and distribution in Minneapolis, one by well-known criminal Mose Barnett and the other at Hect's (Hecht's?) Cigar Store in Minneapolis.

Drug prices were high with morphine selling for $100 an ounce, heroin for $120 an ounce, yen shee (the residue left from smoking opium in a pipe) at $35 an ounce, and cocaine fluctuating between $65 and $75 an ounce. The largest number of opium addicts, according to the narcotics agent in charge of Minneapolis, were white women of the better class.

Furs

The *Grand Forks Herald* reported in its February 11, 1915, issue on a downtown smuggling ring based out of an unnamed Minneapolis saloon. The resolute George E. Foulkes, special agent for the U. S. Treasury Department, tracked down the $100,000 business headed by fur smugglers. John and C. F. Kirk worked with local pawn brokers to redistribute the stolen furs around the country.

The goods were shipped out of Winnipeg, Canada, and were reportedly stolen from the Hudson Bay Company, Holt-Renfrew Company, Eaton Company and the Boler Waugh Company. All bought their wares from traders in the far northern part of Canada and conducted extensive exporting businesses.

Minnesota Loan and Trust Company held smuggled jewels.
Photo courtesy of the Hennepin County Library.

Jewelry

In a show of bad form, local millionaire Hiram A. Lyon, head of several Minneapolis banks (articles differ on whether Lyon was a banker or a grain dealer), was arrested in New Jersey for smuggling two pearl necklaces, a brooch and a gold watch into the U.S. from Europe after a family trip. Lyon and his wife were taken to Hoboken where he posted $2,500 bail in cash. He was later arraigned in Trenton, New Jersey, on June 2, 1910, and fined $5,000. Newspapers derided the bank president for his attempt to defraud the government, seeing no difference between his actions and those of criminals who might rob his banks.

As it turned out, Minneapolis was home to an extensive jewelry smuggling ring which lasted for roughly a decade. The ring was uncovered in the early 1900s when a suitcase of jewels, reportedly smuggled across the Canadian border from Manitoba, was discovered inside the vaults of the Minnesota Loan and Trust Company. Tipped off by an anonymous letter, government agent George E. Foulkes was hot on the trail of the traffickers who transported goods via the Northern Pacific

Wealthy jewelry smugglers lived at the Leamington Hotel in Minneapolis.
Photo courtesy of the Hennepin County Library.

Railroad. An additional $50,000 worth of jewelry was located at the Northwestern Bank.

The smugglers were reported to be wealthy men and women who made their homes in the Leamington Hotel where they systematically smuggled costly jewels and clothing. Additional tips were provided by the smugglers' competitors, legitimate businessmen and business women who claimed they could not compete against members of the ring.

In 1912, The *Evening Times* reported that $3,000 worth of diamonds, watches, rugs, rings and laces were seized at the home of a prominent Minneapolis resident working with a local organized crime syndicate.

Checks for payment of the goods were also found. The *Times* reported that several St. Paul men, recognized in business and social circles and stockholders in the Minneapolis jewelry firm involved in the smuggling case, made large payments to United States customs officials to settle the matter. The names of the men and the jewelry business were carefully guarded from the public. The men declared their innocence, suggesting that they had only attended stockholder meetings and had no knowledge of illegal activity.

The smuggling system used by this Minneapolis jeweler called for sending a representative to the firm's London agency for a specific amount of jewelry. After taking possession of the jewelry, the representative would connect with agents in Winnipeg who would advise him if he could safely cross the border without detection, thus avoiding paying a duty on the merchandise. If the representative was suspected of being shadowed, the jewelry would be handed off to another agent. That courier would ferry the jewelry across the border into Minnesota and straight to Minneapolis for deposit. He would then prepare for another trip across the ocean. Once the jewelry was deposited at one of the banks, it was then distributed throughout the Northwest. Investigators believed the operators of the smuggling ring worked out of New York. The U.S. Treasury Department refused to discuss details of the case, other than confirming that seizures had been made in Minneapolis.

Poodle Girl

The *Minneapolis Journal* reported in October of 1900 that a beautiful young opera singer, Evangeline Lyons, was arrested in Star Lake, Wisconsin, after smuggling diamonds through Minneapolis from France, via Halifax and Montreal. She accomplished this feat by starving a pet poodle while in Montreal, then feeding it chunks of diamond-embedded fat. According to the article, the dog was starved "until willing to eat anything without asking questions."

Lyons was arrested by Special Customs Officers, who charged her with smuggling $25,000 worth of diamonds on her last trip. She smuggled goods valued at more than $100,000 during her career.

The *Minneapolis Journal* took special note of Lyons' accomplice, Norman Lees, who remained in France to purchase diamonds. Lees had apparently worked as a reporter in Minneapolis years earlier and was considered a "decidedly unsophisticated specimen of a needy and newly arrived Briton" during his Minneapolis stay. The article suggested that Lees never would have been suspected of possessing enough cleverness to carry out such a crime.

He had most recently relocated from Minneapolis to Chicago, where he was compiling a list of disreputable houses in which to present a play, *If Christ Came to Chicago.*

Special Customs Agents visited Minneapolis earlier looking for Lyons, a member of the "Clifford's Gaiety Girls." She was noted, as one of America's beauties, to "cut a wide swath," with an irreproachable figure in tights at the Omaha exhibition In this capacity, Lyons met a "certain speculative New Yorker" who was known to deal extensively in gems, selling them to dealers from Boston to San Francisco. Investigators could only speculate on whether the fine figure of Lyons, or a cold, hard business arrangement, caught the man's attention.

The young woman and the elderly man booked passage to France though the Cunard Agency. Less than two weeks later Lyons returned by way of Halifax to the United States, eventually making five such trips from Liverpool to Halifax, then onto the United States via Canada. On her last trip, she was followed from Halifax to Montreal where she stayed at St. Lawrence Hall. She suddenly headed west on the Canadian Pacific Railway, then took the Soo Line to the Twin Cities with the customs men on her trail. They reported that she was very gracious the entire route and traveled with only a small hand satchel and no other baggage. She had, as a companion, a sweet little Japanese poodle.

At the boundary line Lyons was searched by a female customs officer who checked every article of clothing. Once in the Twin Cities she was driven from the depot to the Ryan hotel where she stayed overnight. She left on the train for Chicago, staying overnight in Wisconsin where her dog became ill and died. The customs agents believe the young woman poisoned the poodle and recouped the gems.

Grain

The *Wilkes-Barre Times* announced on October 10, 1911, that a grain smuggling ring was being run by several wealthy Minneapolis millers. Walter Jackson, wheat buyer for The Atlantic Grain Company, and A.J. Magnie, a farmer, were accused of smuggling grain across the border from Canada at night. The grain was then deposited on Minnesota farms and transported to elevators near the border.

Smuggled barley garnered a four-cent per bushel price gain, the grain price difference between the U.S. and Canada. The profit was then split between the producer, the American farmer and the grain buyer. According to Special Customs Agent Foulkes thousands of bushels of

Hauling grain in the Minneapolis Mill District in the late 1800s.
Photo courtesy of the Hennepin County Library.

wheat were shipped to Minneapolis flour mills every year from Canada with no duty paid.

The article concluded that the smuggling operations were discovered by accident when federal officers were searching the border for the lost painting, Mona Lisa, which had been stolen from the Louvre in France on the morning of August 21, 1911.

Humans

At the turn of the 20th Century, the United States border patrol was trying to cut back on Chinese men being smuggled by white criminals over the Canadian border into the United States. The practice was well-known by government officials, but worth the risk to the smugglers as each Chinaman was worth $500. Minneapolis was listed as a popular dumping ground where the victims were consigned to agents for organized crime, concealed and distributed across the country. They were then put to work with a portion of their wages repaid to organized crime for the cost of importation. If the agent was found out and his cargo discovered, he lost out on the $500 lump sum bonus for his work on behalf of the smuggling ring.

Once in Minneapolis, the Chinese were disguised as workers in laundries and restaurants run by fellow countrymen. Boarding houses received good pay for harboring the victims until they were distributed to their destinations. They travelled dressed in American garb and under the cover of darkness. The unsuspecting victims paid their smugglers good money to pass them into the hands of organized crime. It was a hazardous arrangement. There were reports of ship's captains ordering Chinese to "walk the plank" when their vessels were in danger of being captured and searched by customs agents.

The railroads carried the smuggled victims, stowed away in boxcars, over the Canadian border to Minneapolis. Agents notified local organized crime when a railcar was expected, making certain they knew the number of the car holding their illegal cargo. Without the complicity of employees at the local rail yards, smuggling would have been impossible. Many a brakeman was able to make an extra bit of cash in the arrangement.

For smuggled Chinamen discovered by authorities and facing deportation back to China, local Chinese merchants were often willing to claim them as their sons. This gave them the right to remain in the country. The father-in-general was paid for his generosity. And though Chinese merchants were considered among the most honest in the U. S., it was accepted wisdom that they considered it a virtue to "beat" the U. S. Government. This trait was explained as a result of years of unfair treatment suffered at the hands of the Chinese government against its own people.

Once the worker decided to return to China, having made enough money to allow him to marry and start raising a family, he secured free passage by selling his immigration papers back to organized crime. The papers had a set market value. When the worker was detected without papers, he allowed himself to be turned in to authorities. He would be found guilty of not having proper documentation and would be sent back to China on the government's dollar.

CHAPTER 6
GAMBLING

Wrongful Death

Mr. X received a letter from Al Capone's great niece and writer, Deidre Marie Capone, in which she complains about trying to straighten out the facts in books and articles about her great uncle, noting that the authors, "and they are all men," don't like to be wrong. (My note: There are certain universal truths women must face, whether we are the nieces of mobsters or the daughters of Minnesota farmers.) The letter either supports evidence of Mr. X's ties to the mob or is an elaborate ruse to make me believe him.

Truth be told, I've read a report of civil suits filed against Mr. X, including a disturbing wrongful death case. So, if he isn't a mobster, he is, at the very least, a man to be reckoned with.

My friends and family worry about my safety while working on this book. Yet, if they ever met Mr. X, they would find him every bit as brilliant and, dare I say, charming as I do. Charm goes a long way when committing fraud. Brains don't hurt either.

In her letter, Capone states that her book, Uncle Al Capone, has been on the bestseller list at Barnes & Noble.com and Amazon.com. Let's face it. Criminals are fascinating people.

Gambling

Hennepin Avenue in the late 1800s was home to many illegal gambling establishments. Photo courtesy of the Hennepin County Library.

"Annual joke – County Attorney of Hennepin begins war to ban gambling in Minneapolis."
Bemidji Daily Pioneer dated December 14, 1922

Gambling drifted up the Mississippi River to Minnesota from its origins in New Orleans in the mid -1800s. As early as the 1850s, other parts of the country recognized the Twin Cities as fertile ground for gambling opportunities.

Four small Minnesota resorts catered to gamblers who journeyed up the Mississippi during the summer months. The most famous was a clubhouse owned by Cole Martin and Cole (King Cole) Conant. Here games of Faro and two billiard tables were available. If Keno was your game, you were in luck. George Devol, who lost his bankroll at the Faro table, borrowed money from Martin and set up a Keno game on the premises. That met with immediate success and paid 10 percent to the house. The game expanded south to Winona, where an abundance of immigrants landed on their way to the northwestern U.S. after the purchase of the Louisiana Territory. Gambling also expanded to the north woods of Minnesota near Brainerd, Moorhead and other communities along the Northern Pacific Railroad.

Minneapolis exported to Chicago what Herbert Asbury referred to in his book, *Sucker's Progress,* as "corn-fed tricksters." The city's gambling business was run by a group of men known as "the combination." They ran gambling houses on Nicollet and Hennepin Avenues. "The combination" was led by John Flanagan and included members Colonel Bill Tanner, Pat Sullivan, Frank Shelly, Mike Shaw and Bill Munday.

The city's pool halls, gambling dens and houses of ill-repute were frequented by drifters. They were often homeless young men camping along the shores of the Mississippi or workers employed by the titans of industry with claims to the land. They cleared forests, laid steel rails and built flour mills as the Twin Cities were molded into a mighty axis of commerce.

Bohemian Flats along the Mississippi River in Minneapolis where the poor and homeless lived. Photo courtesy of the Hennepin County Library.

The *Minneapolis Journal* carried an editorial on October 3, 1895, written by W. G. Calderwood, secretary of the state Prohibition Committee, which drew attention to the inequity in Minneapolis' gambling culture based on race. Calderwood also suggested that individuals in Republican Mayor Robert Pratt's administration had ties to organized crime. He wrote:

> It is hard to read that seven colored men have been arrested and one of them fined for gambling under the administration of the mayor and chief of police, both of whom have brilliant records as veterans in the late war for freedom of the slave. Where is the glorious 15th amendment for which the officers just above mentioned fought and bled? Where are the boasted rights of the colored man, and his vaunted equality before the law, if he cannot gamble, syndicate or no syndicate?
>
> Laying aside all joking, why is it that a certain coterie of men in this city are allowed to run gambling houses year in and year out, with no effort on the part of the police to restrain them, while anyone who has not the sanction of this so-called syndicate is very summarily dealt with, whether he be a white man from Kansas City or a black man from Minneapolis?
>
> It is useless, in view of the boldness with which the gambling industry is carried on in this city, for any intelligent man to say that we have not crime – organized, protected crime – in this city. Such organized, protected crime, under exactly the same circumstances, in other cities, has always been found, upon investigation to be inseparably connected with organized official corruption. The surface indications being the same in Minneapolis, is it not about time for some one in official circles, who knows, or ought to know, to inform the public – whose servant he is – what the difference is, if indeed, there be any difference, between organized, systematic protection of crime in New York or Chicago? If any difference exists, let some honest officer arise and enlighten the public on its distinguishing characteristics.
>
> -W.G. Calderwood

W. G. Calderwood, secretary of the state Prohibition Committee. Photo courtesy of the Hennepin County Library.

Minneapolis was host to a variety of businesses serving up vices in the 1920s and 30s, with Big Mose Barnett's gambling establishment at 820 Hennepin Avenue and Danny Hogan's joint at 208 11th Avenue South. Hennepin County Attorney Floyd B. Olson's investigators, Melvin Passolt and Frank Brunskill, appeared unable to locate and shut down those illegitimate businesses – or others, like the game run by Hank Gardner at the Buford Hotel; or Dahl's place; or the gambling rooms of Ed Lewis and Chappie Johnson at the Ranier Hotel. Chinese gambling joints also operated at Fourth Avenue South. A huge game carried on by Eddie Randall employed twenty "runners" with drawings twice a day at a well-known downtown hotel.

Jack Keffler was the collector for the slot machine syndicate. His weekly take was estimated at not less than $7,000. Twenty-five percent of that was distributed to the owner of the slot machine site, 50 percent to the machine owners, and the remaining 25 percent split to pay for protection. According to underworld rumors, William Appelt, a relative by marriage of County Attorney Olson, and Art Goff, brother to Assistant Hennepin County Attorney Edward Goff, were closely connected with the control of slot machines.

Big Mose Barnett. Photo courtesy of the
Hennepin County Library, Minneapolis Collection, M271.

In addition to slot machines, punch boards were prohibited by law. They were, however, plentiful during the 1920s and 30s with at least 2,500 distributed throughout Minneapolis. Punch board owners received 60 percent of the profits. The punch boards were manufactured by Hamilton Manufacturing Company, which monopolized their production and placement. Unless a punch board was manufactured by Hamilton, whose president was A. Weiss, police would insist upon its removal.

In the 1920s, Tommy Banks took over the gaming industry in Minneapolis. An understanding between the authorities and the underworld in Minneapolis was documented in an article critical of then Minnesota Governor Floyd B. Olson. V. F. Calverton wrote in the January 1936 *Modern Monthly* magazine:

> Anyone who has spent any time in Minneapolis knows, from personal observation, if not experience, that there are few cities in

the United States where gangsterism rules with such an obvious hand, or with such complete contempt of all authority. Although there are more murders per day in Chicago than in Minneapolis (and until recently, St. Paul) they operate with more freedom, and make their presence felt in everyday life more conspicuously than they ever dared to do in Chicago.

If Olson has nothing to with the gang world, as his friends contest, then why has he never made any attempt to rid the state of the gangsters who strut up and down the streets of Minneapolis, run the slot-machine racket, the night-club racket, the prostitution racket, and make life impossible for everyone or anyone who dares defy their power?

. . . Olson is not interested in fighting racketeers and gangsters, because too many of his political henchmen are tied up with them in their various activities."

Investigator Melvin Passolt.
Photo courtesy of the Hennepin County Library.

Sports Betting

In the early 1930s, two Minnesota men became famous as odds makers using a new type of statistic called the point spread form of handicapping in sports betting. The point spread method guaranteed a profit for bookies, enabling more bettors to win on any given team. Darby Hicks was a handicapper at the *Minneapolis Journal* during the Great Depression. Karl Ersin, impressed with Hicks' work and being a numbers man himself, made his way to the *Minneapolis Tribune* to ask if they could use a handicapper. It turned out they could, and Hicks began contributing a weekly article. The two men had a friendly rivalry going, predicting the winners.

Ersin met and befriended Billy Hecht, a Minneapolis liquor store owner. The two got to talking about betting. According to the book, *Betting the Line: Sports Wagering in American Life*, Hecht was lured out of Chicago by Leo Hirschfield to create the "Minneapolis Line." In 1937, Hecht was in the process of starting the *Gorham Press*, provding gamblers with a "bible" for betting. It became the first national odds making institution and set a countrywide standard. Several hundred subscribers could phone Ersin and Hecht's offices during the week for any minor adjustments on upcoming games.

In 1940, Hirschfield bought into the publication and changed the name of the company to *Athletic Publications*. The newsletter was renamed the *Weekly Gridiron Review*, affectionately referred to as the *Green Sheet*. Hirschfield eventually added additional features and stories to his magazine which broadened its appeal. Although most of his customers were illegal bookmakers, Hirschfield's business was completely legitimate.

Ersin suspected that professional games were being fixed during the 1930s and 40s when bets were loaded with what he termed "unnatural" money. But he couldn't confirm his suspicions related to an abundance of winners.

Subscribers paid about $25 per week for information. *The Green Sheet* grew in popularity and, although it employed fewer than twenty people, its annual gross income was almost $10,000,000. Ersin lauded Hirschfield as being a "totally honest man" who steered clear of shady associations. But the same wasn't necessarily true of his employees.

In 1948, Mort Olshan, joined Hirschfield's magazine as a statistician at $90 a week, after reading a *Collier's* magazine article about Hirschfield entitled "The Wizard of Odds." Within a month his weekly wages increased to $100 and several months later to $115. This was a considerable amount of money for a 22-year-old man back then.

Olshan, a Buffalo, New York, native, had just returned from serving in Okinawa during World War II when he moved to Minneapolis. As a child he booked nickel and dime action, betting on the Niagara basketball team. Olshan had a gift for numbers. He left the company and Minnesota in the 1950s and began *The Gold Sheet* in California.

The *Green Sheet* handicappers worked independently, digesting sports news from forty different newspapers. They did the bulk of their work on weekends, after analyzing college and professional game statistics. They then set their lines, giving bettors an idea of how much money they should risk in order to win on a team. Olshan claimed he never met Hecht, who worked in partnership with Joe Numero in the bookmaking operation. They operated separately from the handicappers.

In 1946, Bert Bell became the National Football League commissioner and introduced legislation making it illegal to fix games. He also wrote an anti-gambling resolution to the League constitution; that was immediately approved. Bell began calling bookmakers and gamblers, especially the Minnesota crew, to detect the possibility of any fixes. According to Bell's son, Upton, his father had a phone line dedicated specifically to bookmakers who worked for underworld operators Meyer Lansky, Frank Costello and Sylvester Corrolla. He helped the mob determine if a sporting event was fixed and heavily bet on in another part of the country. Such action could result in a possible swindle.

The Hirschfield Company was undermined by new laws created in the early 1960s under U.S. Attorney General Robert F. Kennedy. Those laws prohibited the sending of odds, wagers or gambling paraphernalia across state lines under maximum penalty of a $10,000 fine and two to five years in prison.

Senate investigators, in 1961, called Hirschfield to testify at a hearing looking into the alleged efforts of gamblers to corrupt college football. He invoked the 5th Amendment when asked about his business. But Hirschfield testified that he was not connected with organized crime and denied the existence of a gambling syndicate. He later defended himself, stating he did not run a gambling institution, but admitting most of his customers were bookmakers. Hecht, the established bookmaker, was also the subject of government investigations.

Hirschfield told investigators that he had an agreement with Maurice Podoloff, president of the National Basketball Association, to warn him of any anomalies in the betting lines that might indicate fraud. Podoloff testified that Hirschfield's nerve center could sniff out any unusual betting activity and that he would be alerted when a fix might be in. Hirschfield had the same agreement with Bell at the NFL. The committee ordered Hirschfield to turn over his client list and the names of any other colleges with whom he communicated. Since almost every point spread in America was broadcast over the wire from Minnesota, there was no way for the company to stay viable. The odds making business closed down, replaced by the publication of hunting and fishing books.

Gambling in "Little Italy"

In northeast Minneapolis stands a tiny family grocery store on the corner of Northeast Spring Street and Northeast Filmore which reportedly once served as the front for all bookie operations in the city during the 1940s and 50s. According to an aged Minneapolis bookie, gamblers late in paying their debts were severely beaten in the basement of the grocery store. The bookie told Mr. X that Frank Schullo was the boss with William C. "Buddy" Wolk as the second in command. Police were paid off with protection money to "look the other way" in this "Little Italy" neighborhood, he said.

Schullo passed the bookie business on to his protégé, Jack Capra, who grew up in northeast Minneapolis' "Dogtown." Capra, in turn, taught his skills to George Patterson. The two eventually took over the city of Minneapolis for the New York based Genovese Crime Family as the Capra-Patterson syndicate. Despite police protection, an informer blew the whistle on the gambling ring which handled over $150,000 a week in bets on sporting events.

Peter Cohen, an odds maker for the former *Green Sheet* who was also known as "Pigskin Pete" or "Pete the Picker," was arrested along with twenty-one other people in a gambling raid by the FBI. The arrests, which took place in June 1971, included twenty-two Twin Cities residents, as well as individuals in Boston, Las Vegas and Europe. Fifty federal agents and local lawmen participated in the arrests after telephones were tapped during a two-month investigation. Police found multiple phones and gambling equipment.

Under the 1955 federal anti-gambling statute, before any defendant could be found guilty, the government must establish beyond a reasonable doubt:

> 1) That a gambling business was conducted in the State of Minnesota;
>
> 2) That the business violated the laws of the State of Minnesota;
>
> 3) That the business had a gross revenue of at least $2,000 in any single day;
>
> 4) That there were five or more persons who did "conduct, finance, manage, supervise, direct or own all or a part of a gambling business."

Steve Thomas, Frank Schullo and Anthony Petrangelo were convicted of a single violation of 18 U.S.C. 1955, which prohibits conducting an "illegal gambling business." Wolk and Capra admitted conducting an illegal bookmaking operation in Minneapolis, laying off bets and exchanging line information on sporting events.

CHAPTER 7
UNIONS AND ORGANIZED CRIME

A Call From Mr. X

Mr. X phoned recently. He calls from different numbers, none of which, apparently, are his own. He asked if I was still working on the book about Minneapolis' underworld that he encouraged me to write. He also alerted me to a change in venue.

"Oh yes, I certainly am," I told him. I squeeze in a few sentences on the keyboard before heading to work in the morning. I am nearly done, although I could write about so much more.

I had been wondering about Mr. X as he disappeared for a while after shutting down the old (and, I assume, illegal) business he revived for his girlfriend. Just what that business was remains a mystery to me. Never mind.

There had been word on the street of a sting operation by the Minneapolis Police Department, Mr. X said. Some time afterward, he sent a letter instructing me to mail future correspondence to a new address. His mail would be forwarded to him, or he would pick it up, or something like that. He assured me that if I sent a letter to the old address, it would not be forwarded. You also must address it to a "Ms.

J.," he told me, then laughed and said he'd had a sex change. OK. Whatever.

He sent me background information on a 1963 murder case in which St. Paul lawyer Eugene Thompson hired a hit man to kill his wife in order to claim a large life insurance payout. Mr. X. claims some guy nicknamed "Swifty," who hung out at the Chi-Lake Bar and Pool Hall and Emil's Bar and Pool Hall, contracted the murderers for Thompson. If you wanted to connect with any nefarious character in the underworld, Mr. X said, you went to Swifty. A client of Thompson told him to get in touch with Swifty, Mr. X said. Occupational hazard, I suppose.

Mr. X described Swifty as a tall, lean sleaze ball with jet-black hair and hunched over shoulders who never spoke above a whisper and always seemed to be looking over his shoulder.

Swifty played billiards and was the go-between for professional criminals and financial sponsors from the straight world in Minneapolis. I suppose he must be dead by now. Mr. X doesn't know his real name. Still, it is an interesting bit of underworld history.

Time to hit the shower and head to work. Mine is a busy life. But it's great as long I do what I'm supposed to and keep my nose clean.

Organized Crime and Minnesota Labor

> The rights which labor has won, labor must fight to protect.
> — Floyd B. Olson

In 1903, a powerful anti-union group, Citizens' Alliance, originated in Dayton, Ohio, as part of the local employers' association. Its name was carefully chosen to reflect the average man. In reality, though, the organization referred to banking institutions and industrial magnates. Considered an antidote to labor unions, the organization went national with a convention in Chicago. At that meeting, the group created the Citizen's Industrial Association of America.

In his fascinating and revealing book, *A Union Against Unions: The Minneapolis Citizens Alliance and Its Fight Against Organized Labor*, William Millikan conveys the truth of the matter spoken by Minnesota anti-labor leader David M. Parry who admitted:

> "(the country) was engaged in a war between the owners of American industry and the working class."

Minneapolis, which was being run by a heavily Republican and business-centric administration, founded a chapter of the Citizens' Alliance in 1908 headed by president A. W. Strong and supported by the city's wealthy families. The Alliance was willing to destroy employers who recognized and worked with labor unions. This was accomplished by boycotting those sympathetic businesses, with banks then threatening to withhold their credit. The Alliance had agreements with local judges and politicians to support business and to tamp down the cooperation of workers attempting to secure living wages.

At the turn of the century, Minneapolis employers paid workers some of the lowest wages in the country. The Citizens' Alliance intended to keep it that way. World War I, however, worked briefly in the unions' favor. The government, aware that employee strikes would slow down much needed production in factories for fighting the war, provided government protection. President Woodrow Wilson appointed financier and philanthropist, Bernard Baruch, as an advisor to work on economic and foreign policy. Baruch saw the need for unity between labor and management as a vital component of national security. Coining the term "Cold War," he pointed out that the enemy could be found abroad, and at home, and they would find discord between labor and management working in their favor. He believed that world peace was the goal of our political system and that our nation could renew itself both physically and spiritually if it worked together. As the need for military-related products grew, so did unions, briefly, during the 1920's.

At the end of WWI, the industrial class of Minneapolis and its bankers launched an attack on employee unions, creating an environment which was tolerant of "open shops" only. Unions experienced a steady loss of employees throughout the close of the decade. But the opposing forces in Minneapolis would eventually meet and the police would be directed to use cold-blooded murder, sanctioned by the business community, to make the unions heel.

Governor Olson Stands With Unions

Farmer-Labor Governor Floyd B. Olson was a union man, believing that working together in cooperation with one's neighbor would benefit a larger number of the state's citizens than endeavoring to secure individual fortune for a few entitled families. He was elected to a conservative legislature which fought against programs designed to benefit the majority of the state's population. When push came to shove, and the wealthy Citizens' Alliance was willingly using violence to cower labor, Olson did not back down.

Minneapolis was a major hauling and distribution center in the 1930s and, at the time, truckers were largely unorganized by the business community. The country was going through the Great Depression and Local 574 of the International Brotherhood of Teamsters began working under the leadership of Vince Dunne to organize the trucking industry. The teamsters met great resistance from the right wing political elements in the city. Despite conservatives' efforts to prevent organization by the city's workers, by 1934, over five thousand truckers had joined the union.

The Minneapolis business community and the Citizens' Alliance had become accustomed to beating the working class, successfully crushing union activity for decades. But the austerity which had been foisted onto the working class by fast and loose regulations in the banking industry sparked a civil war. The working class had reached the end of its tether and would no longer tolerate the tyranny inflicted by Minneapolis' elite.

In May of that year, truckers began a strike for increased wages, shorter work hours and the right to represent "inside" workers who ran the offices, warehouses and distribution centers. With business refusing to work with the union, the truckers shut down the system and patrolled the streets to make sure no "scab" drivers were taking their places.

The striking truckers' wives formed an auxiliary group, showing solidarity with their husbands and, at times, fighting with police. During the showdown, no trucking was allowed except by permit and absolute necessity. Farmers and workers worked cooperatively to establish markets for the distribution of food, leaving middlemen out of the arena. Thirty-five thousand building workers also walked out on their jobs in protest of police violence authorized by the business community.

Federal intervention was requested by Governor Olson. He reportedly met with President Franklin D. Roosevelt and asked his administration to impress upon the Citizens' Alliance of Minneapolis that it would be in their best interest to settle the strike if they planned on benefiting from the funds set aside for the Reconstruction Finance Corporation. This independent agency of the United States government was established in 1932 to loan money to banks and businesses that might otherwise have failed.

On May 25, workers returned to their jobs after the governor helped mediate their demands. Within a few weeks, though, business owners were not abiding by the terms of the agreement. On July 17, workers struck again. Three days later, a large group of unarmed strikers were shot at by one hundred police officers after they were lured into the street by deputies riding in a scab truck. Two men were killed and over sixty-five injured. A public commission concluded, after hearing testimony, that police took direct aim at the unarmed pickets and fired to kill. Olson declared martial law.

In a last desperate move, business owners comprising the Alliance announced on the radio that laborers were concealing arms in union headquarters. The National Guard was dispatched to search for arms, but found none. This infuriated Olson, who then turned the tables and sent the National Guard to raid Citizens' Alliance headquarters. They ransacked the office, confiscating papers and files.

In the end, the union workers won the bloody strike. The *Minneapolis Labour Review* carried an article which noted:

> "The winning of this strike marks the greatest victory in the annals of the local trade union movement ... it has changed Minneapolis from being known as a scab's paradise to being a city of hope for those who toil."

Olson was eventually compelled to bring a case against the Citizens' Alliance after the organization hired a hit man to dynamite the home of a union leader.

Organized Crime Exploits Unions

With a steady stream of union dues, local organized crime members constructed various frauds to impose upon local business, thus securing a cut of the action. One of the first documented cases of union racketeering in Minneapolis occurred during the mid-1920s. Thousands of small businessmen within Minneapolis and St. Paul were coerced into paying "dues" for the privilege of belonging to fake unions. The ruse was patterned after Al Capone's Chicago gang.

The celebrated "Dry Cleaners' Case" was brought to the public's attention after Sam Shapiro, who ran a dry cleaning establishment at 2615 East Franklin Avenue in Minneapolis, was assaulted because he refused to pay up.

Shapiro was hit over the head with a revolver and the assailants sprayed corrosive acid on the clothing left in his care, causing roughly $12,000 in damages. He reported the attack to Hennepin County Attorney Floyd B. Olson, complaining that a few days earlier Big Mose Barnett and Phillip Moses had approached the dry cleaner, claiming to represent the Dry Cleaners Association, and tried to intimidate him into joining the group.

Surprisingly, Olson took no action, even though a grand jury in the Dry Cleaners Case was in session. Olson acted only after private citizen and publisher J. M. Near, editor of *The Saturday Press*, advised Grand Jury Foreman J. J. Fehr of the incident and assaults on other dry cleaners.

When he received the letter, Foreman Fehr met with Shapiro to collect details of the crime. The grand jury took up the case and, as a result, sixty-four individuals and seventeen firms were indicted for conspiracy in restraint of trade. The assailants were indicted for first degree assault.

The indicted gunmen were Harry Jaffa, Paul Gottlieb and Abe Jankowitz. The day after the indictments were announced, Jaffa and Gottlieb were involved in the shooting of Near's partner, newspaper editor Howard Guilford.

Still, months went by without any effort by Hennepin County Attorney Olson to prosecute the mob. The known gunmen were never required to face a jury. When Shapiro began the process of starting a civil suit against the criminals, a settlement was effected for $8,700. According to a report by Walter Liggett in the *Midwest American* newspaper, Olson acted more as a referee whose main interest appeared to be preventing Shapiro from proceeding with criminal charges against the man who bashed him in the head with a gun.

Sam Shapiro attacked in dry cleaner's racketeering case. Photo courtesy of Mark Evans.

After the grand jury returned indictments, Olson was credited for the jury's success. Newspapers published statements in which the county attorney promised wholesale convictions. In reality, nearly a year after things had simmered down, only seven officers and directors of the fraudulent Twin Cities Dry Cleaners Association paid fines ranging from $500 - $1,000.

Then, on December 30, 1930, as he was assuming the office of governor, Olson dismissed the remaining eighty-one indictments without the dry cleaners' case ever going to trial. He defended his actions by saying he count not collect sufficient, convincing evidence connecting the defendants to the violence. Olson also claimed the cost of a trial would be too great.

Labor Racketeering in the 1950s

In 1954, a house committee probed alleged racketeering charges in Minneapolis. Three Minneapolis businessmen testified about their payments to American Federation of Labor Teamster unions to avoid labor troubles at their firms. They suggested teamster officials showed a pattern of misusing their power to build more power. The committee claimed employers paid union bosses to prevent strikes and picket lines.

One witness accused a teamster local of not even holding elections, dragging employees into union membership without their knowledge. Another witness said a picket line was placed around his business because teamsters wanted to organize employees, even though employees themselves had not expressed an interest in unionizing.

The union was headed by Tony Schullo, a friend of local organized crime members Rocky Lupino and John Azzone. Their relationship is memorialized in a1953 photograph, now archived at the Minnesota Historical Society, of the three on a fishing trip. Schullo, then secretary-treasurer of the AFL Teamsters' Miscellaneous Drivers' Local 648, said he "organized" this way. He then went on, charging employees with "unfair labor practices." Schullo's thinking about unionization was somewhat convoluted as illustrated by this unusual exchange between Representative Hoffman and Schullo:

> Mr. Hoffman: What employees were unfair to your organization?
> Mr. Schullo: The ones that didn't belong.

Mr. Hoffman: Anyone that doesn't belong to your organization is unfair?

Mr. Schullo: That's right.

The testimony went on to illustrate how Schullo used unwarranted economic power to harm a business, and the union's own dues-paying members. Minneapolis businessmen at times paid the teamsters leaders directly to protect them from a picket line or strike, removing the rights of the employees to demonstrate for higher wages. Through collusion between the teamsters and the business community, labor laws were completely side-stepped.

As the owner of Associated Activities Company in Minneapolis, Sylvester Cargill testified he paid $500 to Eddie Blixt of Teamsters' Local 544 for "initiation fees." Cargill later paid $2,000 to Local 648 Secretary-Treasurer Schullo because he feared union violence.

Donald Gabbert of Gabbert Radio and Television Sales said he paid teamsters $306 to pull picketers from his business in December 1950. In addition, Andrew Mollner, general manager of Palm Beach Cosmetics Company, paid $30 per month to Local 548 for protection from labor problems.

Union boss Tony Schullo.
Photo courtesy of the Hennepin County Library.

CHAPTER 8
MINNEAPOLIS JOURNALIST MURDERS

Permission

I received a letter from the publisher of four books related to Minneapolis organized crime and the Baldies street gang. The publisher is, apparently, a friend of Mr. X and the wife of a late organized crime member.

> This letter is giving you permission to use any and all material in the following books ... Do not contact anyone written about in these books – too dangerous.
> I am currently retired now and very sick. My days are now numbered. This will by my first and last contact with you.
>
> Good luck always,
> Sincerely,
> E. J. Johnson

The books are currently carried by the Hennepin County Library. They have a homespun look with plastic bindings and photocopied pages. Yet, they carry the only documented history of Minneapolis' underworld that I have come across thus far.

A torch has been passed to me, of all people. Very well then. This one is for you, Ms. Johnson.

Guilford, Liggett & Kasherman

Collusion between politicians and racketeers was taking place in Minneapolis, but local newspapers were not reporting it. In the shadows lurked a group of intrepid newsmen willing to lay their lives on the line to expose the rottenness eating away at the heart of the city.

If reporters Arthur Kasherman, Howard Guilford, and Walter Liggett were alive today, they would likely publish alternative news blogs. In the 1920s and 30s, Guilford and Liggett worked as investigative journalists and muckrakers. Minnesota politicians, gangsters, police and the local media often derided them as being of unsound mind. They were reporters hell-bent on exposing the truth about the control of organized crime. They hit more than one nerve with their fearless, and sometimes risky, reporting.

The Twin Cities have a history of investigative reporters snooping into the relationships of politicians and organized crime.

In 1927, renegade newspaper publisher J. M. Near, described as anti-Semitic, anti-Catholic, anti-black and anti-labor, accused then Hennepin County Attorney Floyd B. Olson of failing to properly investigate organized crime. Near and one of his reporters, Howard Guilford, an accomplished writer of children's verse and a published author, predicted in their first issue of the *Twin Cities Reporter* that they stood a chance of being "rubbed out" if they went ahead with publication.

Near and Guilford initially worked together, establishing *the Twin Cities Reporter*. It carried headlines like "Smooth Minneapolis Doctor with Woman in St. Paul Hotel" and "White Slaver Plying Trade: Well Known Local Man Ruining Women and Living Off Their Earnings." The paper invariably used common derogatory terms when referring to minorities. The Chinese were "chinks," Italians were "dagos," and African Americans were referred to as "dinges."

It is not clear why, in 1920, the newspaper was sold to underworld figures Mose Barnett, Ed Morgan, Jack Bevans and "Red" Clare. But after the sale, Near and Guilford accused the new owners of using the paper for blackmail purposes and to support the gambling rackets in Minneapolis. The pair pledged to "exterminate" the paper, despite threats made against them. The men naively believed that if anything should happen to them:

> "Old Sir John Law will begin stuffing Stillwater penitentiary full of certain gentlemen and before he finishes, that model institution will be so overcrowded that the last few dozen will have to sleep with their legs out the windows."

Guilford was assaulted on the morning of September 22, 1927, by gunmen as he and his sister-in-law drove to work. Though the first bullet missed his head, when his sister-in-law shoved him aside, another found his stomach. With twenty-nine perforations in his intestine, Guilford was not expected to live. He survived, then faced a second attempt on his life while hospitalized with those initial bullet wounds.

County Attorney Olson was asked to send a representative to the hospital to record Guilford's expected dying statement. Olson flatly refused, explaining that Guilford's car was 100 feet outside of Minneapolis. He also declared Guilford's attack "underworld war," washing his hands of the affair.

According to her book, *Stopping the Presses*, Marda Liggett Woodbury, daughter of murdered newspaper editor Walter Liggett, claims that Minneapolis Chief of Police Frank Brunskill ordered his men to stop at downtown newsstands and command the newsboys not to sell *The Saturday Press* because it was "inciting to riot."

Hennepin County Sheriff Earle Brown brought his own stenographer to Guilford's bedside, collecting the wounded man's statement. That led to the identification of Paul Gottlieb, Harry Jaffa and "Flippy" Scher in connection with the shooting. Guilford later withdrew identifying his attackers in the paper, referring to them instead as "Chicago's cold blooded murderers." Though indicted, the men were never prosecuted. Guilford wrote after the attack:

> "I was told when I refused to accept a weekly envelope from the gambling syndicate in Minneapolis some time ago that I would be bumped off."

Near and Guilford became increasingly provocative with their editorials. Near wrote:

Ninety percent of the crimes committed against society in this city are committed by Jew gangsters. If law abiding Jews wanted to rid themselves of the odium and stigma the rodents of their own race have brought upon them, they need only step to the front and help the decent citizens of Minneapolis rid the city of these criminal Jews.

Guilford also refused to back down, writing that he had been shot by Jews and, as a result, had "withdrawn all allegiance to anything with a hook nose that eats herring."

Publisher Near, along with Guilford and Kasherman, continued publishing inflammatory exposés about the political establishment in Minneapolis, listing the addresses of bootlegging enterprises and gambling houses. They tried to goad law enforcement into raiding such establishments. Rather than raid these places of vice, law enforcement focused on *The Saturday Press*, filing criminal libel charges against *The Saturday Press* with a gag law. That drew the ire of newspapers across the country.

County Attorney Olson had no tolerance for anti-Semitism. And, though he was accused of failing to act on organized crime, he quickly lodged a complaint against publisher Near under the Public Nuisance Law of 1925 – also known as the Minnesota Gag Law. It was an attempt to shut down Near's press.

The law provided permanent injunctions against creating public nuisances by publishing, selling or distributing malicious, scandalous and defamatory newspapers. In 1931, under *Near vs. Minnesota*, the United States Supreme Court 283 U.S. 697 determined the gag law violated the First Amendment to the Constitution. It was the same precedent used by the *New York Times* in 1971 in an attempt to publish the Nixon Administration's *Pentagon Papers*. Porn dealer Ferris Alexander also revived *Near vs. Minnesota* in his court case, claiming a violation of free speech.

Guilford Murder, September 6, 1934

Article from the *Midwest American* entitled "Shotgun Censorship," published by Walter Liggett after Guilford's murder.

After his election as governor, Floyd B. Olson was feeling heat from the Non-Partisan League as it reviewed appointments made by Olson's All-Party machine. That selection group consisted of professional politicians from all three parties, plus liquor and railroad lobbyists. The Non-Partisan League felt Olson was losing the spirit of the Farmer-Labor in its fight to loosen the Republican Party's stranglehold on Minneapolis, by appointing individuals from all parties to key positions.

Newspaper editor Walter Liggett disagreed with Olson's approach to governance, accusing him of working in the interest of underworld figures, brewers, distillers, bankers and recipients of public contracts.

Olson invited Liggett; Arthur Townley, founder of the Non-Partisan League; and several League delegates to lunch on September 5, 1934. Liggett noted that the governor mentioned Howard Guilford's name three times during that meeting, even though no one in the room appeared to know the journalist. Nor did the discussion seem to have any logical connection to Guilford.

Guilford was murdered around 5 p.m. the following day when shots were fired from another vehicle into his car at the intersection of Pillsbury and Ridgewood Avenues in Minneapolis. He appeared to be returning to his apartment at 601 Ridgewood. Guilford died instantly and his car rolled to a halt in a nearby yard. A bag of cakes and cookies rested on the seat next to him and a collection of fishing tackle sat on the back seat. And, on the radio, the last few innings of the Minneapolis-Milwaukee baseball game played.

Upon Guilford's death, Liggett wrote:

> Ordinarily, when a newspaper man is murdered by gangsters, the press unites in demanding speedy punishment for its perpetrators. So well established is this precedent that the underworld considers it very "bad business" indeed to knock off anyone connected with the Fourth Estate. But when Howard Guilford was recently shot down in broad daylight on the streets of Minneapolis by paid assassins, the *Farmer-Labor Leader*, (Olson's political party's newspaper) in its first succeeding issue, accused the slain editor of being a blackmailer *and sought to justify his murder. The cue of the Farmer*-Labor Leader was followed by the *Union Labor Advocate* of St. Paul and the next week at least half a dozen Farm-Labor papers throughout the state tried to condone this cold blooded murder by condemning Guilford.

> ...Nevertheless, it is impossible to deny that he performed valuable civic service in uncovering crookedness by police officials and others – and in revealing the racketeering that existed in Minneapolis' underworld. One of his exposures nearly twenty years ago in St. Paul did much towards breaking the control of the O'Connor ring.
>
> Just before his death, Guilford had promised some startling exposures of the ramifications of the Twin City under-world with an attaché of the Olson regime. As a consequence he was decidedly "persona non grata" with the state capital crowd. Shortly after his murder Senator Schall declared it was a case of "shotgun censorship" while A. C. Townley asserted he believed Gov. Olson knew that Guilford's death was impending.
>
> We have no hesitancy in repudiating the insinuations of both Schall and Townley. We do not for one moment believe that Floyd B. Olson is the type of man who would hire gunmen to do away with an opponent. On the other hand, some of Olson's close associates have friends among the denizens of the Twin Cities underworld who ARE that type of men ...

Guilford's murder was never solved by the Minneapolis Police department, and a friend of Guilford and Near, Robert Wilson, told Walter Liggett's daughter years later that he learned about the impending murder the day Guilford was killed, but was unable to warn him. Wilson believed the Minneapolis police department was in on the murder. In contrast, his former partner, Near, believed Guilford was targeted by professional gangsters hired by communists. Guilford was preparing to write a derogatory piece about them, motivated by his opposition to labor unions. He stood defiantly on the side of the Republican Citizens' Alliance.

Liggett Murder, December 9, 1935

Walter Liggett. Photo courtesy of Mark Evans

Walter Liggett had excellent credentials as a journalist and editor, having worked for newspapers around the country. He was born in Benson, Minnesota, where his father managed a 2,000 acre stock farm. At the tail end of the Prohibition era in 1933, Liggett returned to

Minnesota from New York City with his wife and two young children. Both Liggett and Hennepin County Attorney Floyd B. Olson were involved in the progressive Non-Partisan League, which later became the Farmer-Labor Party.

Liggett's relationship with Olson was flavored by a journalistic assignment a decade earlier when he was writing a series about the effects of Prohibition on our country. He uncovered unsavory evidence linking Olson to local organized crime. Liggett was assured by members of the newly formed Farmer-Labor party that Olson had turned over a new leaf. The reporter was willing to give Olson a fair chance to prove himself.

Liggett was considering a position as editor for a Chicago-based national magazine when he met Olson for the first time at the Minneapolis Athletic Club. Liggett was thoroughly charmed by Olson. During that meeting, the two negotiated establishment of a Farmer-Labor newspaper in Rochester, Minnesota, to represent the southeastern part of the state. Olson was integral in arranging funding for a plant and press in the Mississippi River town of Red Wing, giving birth to the *Midwest American*. That newspaper would eventually become Olson's nemesis.

At the demise of Prohibition, then Minnesota Governor Olson crafted a bill that would utilize new liquor taxes to help cover the cost of relief programs for Minnesota residents most hard-hit by the Great Depression. Though some politicians preferred to find relief funding elsewhere, this proved an effective plan.

Liggett was disenchanted with Olson's decision to assign the concession of newly-legal liquor to the public through bootleggers like Kid Cann and Meyer Shuldberg. He preferred instead that the state dispense liquor. Liggett objected to the formerly illegal liquor interests' participation in the legislative process. Such involvement only reinforced his position that the governor was in cahoots with the mob.

The new Minnesota Liquor Control Bill was signed by Olson on January 6, 1934. Former Secretary of State Boxing Commissioner David Arundel was now the new liquor control commissioner, responsible for enforcing regulations regarding the manufacture, distribution, sale and consumption of liquor.

Another point of contention was Olson's tendency to send government printing jobs out of state. Liggett begged Olson to throw some business his way, but the governor responded by telling Liggett:

> "Remember, I'm ambitious and want to go places. I've got to take care of the papers out of the state as well as in the state."

Liggett's newspaper attacks against Olson grew steadily and he seemed determined to prevent him from winning reelection. In the process, he more boldly reported Olson's ties with organized crime. He compared the Olson All-Party machine to Tammany Hall in New York City, the Democratic Party political machine which controlled the city through graft and political corruption. Liggett wrote:

Minneapolis Athletic Club where Governor Floyd B. Olson met with Walter Liggett. Photo courtesy of the Hennepin County Library.

My wife and I have lived for several years in New York City under Tammany Hall and are thoroughly familiar with the underworld tactics of professional spoilsmen.

That is one reason why we object to the Tammanyization of Minnesota by this All-Party group of racketeers. We knew precisely what to expect when we began our expose' of Floyd Olson and his crew of political hatchet-men.

Knowing them as we do, we will be surprised if they stop much short of assassination. One editor, Howard Guilford, has already been shot down in cold blood by hired gunmen because he dared to expose some ramifications of Floyd Olson with the underworld – and to date the much-press-agented State Bureau of Criminal Apprehension hasn't made any headway in tracking down his slayers.

However, I don't think they will have me killed. It wouldn't look good for one thing, and for another thing, the whole damned cowardly crew knows that they can't find one scintilla of evidence to besmirch my professional reputation in an attempt to justify a cold blooded murder as they did in poor Howard Guilford's case.

Liggett was wrong about a possible attempt on his life. After a long day of work, he was mowed down by a Thompson machine gun in cold blood before his wife, Edith, and 10-year-old daughter Marda. The Liggett's 12-year-old son, Wallace, was just yards away, listening to a radio show in apartment 114 at 1825 Second Avenue South in Minneapolis. Liggett had just pulled his automobile into the alley behind their apartment building and parked, with his daughter still in the car. As Liggett was about to lift a bag of groceries out of the back seat, another vehicle turned into the alley. A blast of five gunshots dropped the journalist to the ground. His wife reported seeing the leering face of Kid Cann snarled into a smile as he pulled the trigger firing the round.

A neighbor and securities trader, Harvey Meyers, was heading into the apartment building from the alley at 214 E. 19th Street when he heard gunshots, believing at first it was a backfiring car. When he realized it wasn't, he raced back outside to ask Mrs. Liggett what happened.

"They shot him right through the heart!" she exclaimed.

He saw the body, then ran into the basement at the entrance of the building to phone the police. When Meyers returned upstairs, he heard the Liggett children screaming and saw Liggett lying on his back with a robe tucked under his head. Meyers checked Liggett's pulse. Mrs. Liggett asked if her husband's heart was still beating and, in order to keep her calm, Meyers told her it was, though he found no heartbeat. Liggett was dead.

When questioned about his recollection of the murder, a man who called himself "Isaacson" and who was a frequent visitor at the apartment across the alley from the Liggett's apartment building, hesitated to talk. His real name was Wesley Anderesch and he had done prison time. He was a reluctant witness, frightened that if he identified the gunman in the Liggett murder, he would also be killed. He contacted an attorney who advised him to do his duty and make a statement to the police, which he did, then dropped out of sight.

The head of the State Bureau of Apprehension, Nielson, and the Minneapolis captain of detectives tracked Anderesch down at his family's farm near Kimball, Minnesota. Nielson confronted Anderesch, stating, "Wesley, you saw that murder."

Anderesch admitted he had and gave the following details:

> "I was going out of the rear door of the apartment about 5:35 p.m. and just as I stepped into the alley, an automobile swung into the alley from 18th Street. It almost ran over me and I jumped back and swore at the driver. Down in the alley, the Liggett car was headed toward 18th Street. It was already parked and the lights were shining on the car that nearly struck me. There were two men in the front seat, one hunched over the wheel, his head ducked down as if he were kind of afraid and the other with a machine gun on his lap. The car continued along. A few seconds later, I heard the shots. I saw Liggett fall. He went down in the glare of his own headlights and then the murder car sped out of the alley into 19th Street."

"Who was the man you saw in the front seat with the machine gun?" he was asked.

"It was Kid Cann."

"Are you sure?"

Anderesch was positive because during the time he had spent in the workhouse for defrauding an innkeeper, Cann was serving time for operating a still. Cann waited on Anderesch's table every day.

Anderesch's father told detectives that his son would not remain in hiding and arrangements had been made to bring him back to Minneapolis. But since the men interviewed Anderesch in Kimball, that was no longer necessary.

Upon news of Liggett's murder, Governor Olson introduced legislation requesting the posting of a $2,500 reward for the arrest and conviction of the men who assassinated Liggett. He also requested a thorough investigation. Meanwhile, Senator Thomas D. Schall announced that he would demand a congressional investigation. Schall, who was close to Liggett, had "read Liggett's palm" expecting the reporter would eventually "die with his boots on."

During the Liggett murder trial, one newspaper reported that when the defendant, Isadore Blumenfield, aka Kid Cann, heard his name announced as the individual charged with Liggett's murder, he turned around and smiled at the person sitting behind him. Cann was eventually acquitted.

Liggett had been scheduled to be a star witness on behalf of North Dakota Governor William Langer's defense in a federal conspiracy case. Charges were filed against Langer for requiring state employees to donate to the Non-Partisan League and to the *Leader*, a newspaper owned by high-ranking officials in his administration. He was eventually acquitted.

Kasherman Murder, January 22, 1945

Arthur Kasherman leaving Stillwater Prison. Photo courtesy of Hennepin County Library, Minneapolis Collection, M2714.

Undeterred by the murder of his mentor, Howard Guilford, and by the murder of publisher Walter Liggett only a year later, investigative journalist Arthur Kasherman famously stated in his quest for justice, "I am not afraid to die."

On March 20, 1941, the Minnesota Business Alliance sent a letter from the Kasota Building at 330 Hennepin Avenue in Minneapolis to churches throughout the Twin Cities asking for financial backing from "the decent element" of the city. The Alliance hoped to start a weekly or semi-monthly newspaper "to expose the rotten conditions of the city and show who was behind the scenes of the 'let-down' of law enforcement in Minneapolis." The letter noted Arthur Kasherman as public relations counsel.

Several days later, the group issued a second letter, this time to the foreman of the grand jury in session at the time, and its members, advising them that Elmer F. Hillner, head of the Minneapolis Police Purity Squad, failed to respond to an earlier letter. The Minnesota Business Alliance had requested a raid on two gambling houses within the city, alleging that police were protecting gambling establishments. The letter went on to suggest that no racket could possibly operate on such a wide-open scale without the protection of the police department and other officials.

The problem with allowing rackets such freedom, according to the Alliance, was that illegal enterprises were robbing the community of millions of dollars. That money would otherwise have been spent in legitimate places of business, thus supporting the local economy. The Alliance asked the grand jury to hire its own investigators and prosecutor, paid for by the county.

Clearly, vice was considered an out of control problem by the business community and Kasherman's position within the Minnesota Business Alliance may have been self-serving. Kasherman managed to publish his newspaper, *The Public Press*, which featured exposés on racketeering and the underworld's ties with Minneapolis Mayor Marvin Kline's administration.

He was a thorn in the side of the Kline administration during the reign of Davie "The Jew" Berman and his brother, Charles "Chickie" Berman's, gambling and prostitution enterprise. The Bermans ran the illegal gambling industry in Minneapolis during the 1940s.

The government did not like anyone peeking under its skirts and was eager to shut down Kasherman's publishing operation. The easiest way to muffle him was to put him in prison. The Minneapolis police ran a sting operation in which Kasherman was accused of shaking down a brothel operator at the Dobbs Hotel for $25. Kasherman allegedly threatened to write about her if she didn't pay up. Despite running an illegal business, the madam was able to continue operation without interference by law enforcement.

During the trial, newspapers painted Kasherman as unhinged, reporting that at one point in the trial, he leapt from his chair in an attempt to attack a prosecuting witness. In the end, he was accused of blackmail and sentenced to four years in Stillwater Prison.

Kasherman was born in Russia around 1900, immigrating with his family to the United States at age ten. He grew up in north Minneapolis, stomping grounds of the late Governor Floyd B. Olson and a variety of underworld figures, including Kid Cann. Kasherman, like Cann, once hawked newspapers as a newsboy.

He graduated from North High School and then attended the Minnesota College of Law. His first printing endeavor was a newspaper he called the *Newsboy's Christmas Greeting*. In a sudden about face, Kasherman's law career became expendable when he found himself caught up in a corruption investigation. He was charged with contempt of court for refusing to reveal the details of a gangster's payoff to the local police department. He justified his refusal to turn over information by claiming to be a newspaper man – a prophesy he quickly fulfilled.

On the icy evening of January 22, 1944, 34-year-old Pearl Von Wald, painted by some newspapers as a prostitute, left the Pantages Theater in downtown Minneapolis looking smart in a white overcoat. She hopped into a car driven by her friend Arthur Kasherman. Von Wald had been beaten the night before by her boyfriend, Ray Sullivan, and was still sporting a black eye. The two decided to get something to eat, enjoying a meal of chow mien around 11 p.m. at Hannah's Cafe, 1425 Chicago Avenue. Sullivan, on the other hand, spent a good part of the day waiting to be bailed out of jail by another girlfriend.

Earlier in the day, 44-year-old Kasherman visited the Hennepin County Courthouse to get the names and addresses of grand jurors with the intent of sharing revealing information about Mayor Kline. He also reportedly stopped at the *Star Journal* office to brag about the newest edition of his newspaper, *The Public Press*. The issue, he stated, was going to be a "real dynamite," exposing a dice game on Nicollet Avenue that was sending profits to the mob in Chicago. The men at the paper teased Kasherman that he better watch out, reminding him what happened to Guilford and Liggett.

While Von Wald and Kasherman were dining, Kasherman's tires were slashed. According to Von Wald's statement to investigators, she and Kasherman left the restaurant and got into Kasherman's Oldsmobile. When they tried to drive away, the car's wheels spun and the car wouldn't move. Across the street, loud organ music played at Danny's Bar. A man leaving the restaurant stopped to help push the car further onto the street where it could gain traction. But when he noticed the flat tire, he told Kasherman he couldn't help him.

Pantages Theater attended by Pearl Von Wald the night Kasherman was murdered. Photo courtesy of the Hennepin County Library.

Kasherman's windows were iced up and prevented him from seeing the black sedan that pulled up beside his car, or the man who got out and put a bullet through the left front window, catching Kasherman in the cheek and leaving shards of glass in his face and neck. The bullets kept coming. He slumped onto Von Wald's lap and pushed her out the passenger side door, then climbed out himself. He ran from the vehicle screaming, "Don't shoot; for God's sake don't shoot," shouting a name Von Wald claimed she did not recognize. Additional shots were fired, striking Kasherman in the head and back. The shooter shot several more rounds into the air with one bullet entering a nearby apartment house. The sedan then sped off leaving Kasherman dead on the sidewalk.

When the *Tribune* reported the murder, the newspaper also revealed that Kasherman had predicted his own death. When asked if he was satisfied they were going to get him, Kasherman replied "yes." When asked how they were going to do it, he said he believed it would be the same way Liggett and Guilford were killed, in a drive by shooting.

Mayor Kline offered a $500 reward from his contingency fund for information leading to the arrest of Kasherman's murderer. Following his demise, local law enforcement had nothing good to say about Kasherman. The *Milwaukee Journal* published an article about Kasherman's murder on January 25, 1945, in which police Captain C.E. McKlasky ironically described Kasherman as:

> " … The biggest damned nuisance we ever saw around the city hall. He was a small time shakedown artist – and I mean real small. He was always imagining a lot of gangland murders, always hollering about something being 'wide open.' He was always giving us bum tips and then making excuses when they didn't show anything on investigation. He never had any witnesses to any of the things he claimed, and was always claiming he didn't want to get anyone into trouble."

The article described Kasherman's publication, *The Public Press*, as a dinky four page sheet which carried violent attacks on Mayor Kline. His last paper's headlines screamed, "City Wide Open, Racketeers in Complete Control of the City; Police Department Used as Tool by Mobsters; Unholy Alliance Evident as Dives Run Wide Open."

CHAPTER 9
MINNEAPOLIS ORGANIZED CRIME

Pizza with Mr. X

I received a call on my cell phone from Mr. X while at work and we arranged to meet at a pizzeria in my neighborhood. He promised to be prompt and, sure enough, when I walked in the door he was there with his hand outstretched in friendship. Of course, I cannot be his friend.

We found a corner table where we could talk. Because it could have been challenging for an organized crime figure and a writer raised on a small farm in southwestern Minnesota to agree on a pizza selection, I suggested he order. I believe that no pizza is bad pizza. I was right. The pizza was great and I ate quite a few slices. You can't become a big, sturdy farm girl without a good appetite.

Mr. X proved talkative, for which I was grateful. I asked whether he was still a member of organized crime. Well, only if a good opportunity comes along; otherwise he is essentially retired. He was particularly proud of a recent project now "paying out in aces" and doing very well. It's hard to know if I should be happy for him or ticked off. He's not paying his share of taxes, yet he's driving on roads paid for by me and other taxpayers. And I can't help but wonder if innocent people are losing their money to a brilliant scam. But I am offered no details, and I don't ask for any.

I am curious about Mr. X's background. Why organized crime? Why did he choose that path in life? He said he has an "anti-social personality." Those are the words he used. It doesn't mean he isn't friendly, he explained. It just means he doesn't feel the laws of society apply to him.

I don't know what to say about that.

Kid Cann

Kid Cann (center) after being acquitted in the 1935 murder trial of the Liggett. Courtesy of the Minnesota Historical Society.

Isadore "Kid Cann" Blumenfield was born in Russia in 1901. Two years later his family immigrated to the United States where they settled in the Near North neighborhood of Minneapolis, home to poor and predominately Jewish families. He sold newspapers as a youngster, often using battling other newsboys to make sure he had the best corner for hawking his papers.

Blumenfield was devoted to his family and, as a youth, worked hard to support them. As a preteen, he discovered he could make more money running errands for criminals and prostitutes than selling newspapers. Thus began his association with the seedier class.

It is unclear whether Blumenfield adopted for himself the moniker "Kid Cann" – a name used by a nationally known prize fighter often mentioned in the sports section of newspapers at the turn of the century – or whether it was given to him. He eventually came to despise the name commonly printed in newspapers reporting his crimes. Instead, Blumenfield preferred the moniker "Fergie" or "Doc Ferguson."

Blumenfield earned the title of "Godfather of the Minneapolis liquor industry," cutting his teeth as a ruthless bootlegger during Prohibition. He established a number of stills in the woods near Fort Snelling, where he and his brothers, Harry and Yiddy, produced and sold liquor on the black market.

He also reportedly ran Al Capone's Minnesota 13 liquor from Stearns County. Minnesota 13 was made from a seed corn, with the same name, developed by the University of Minnesota. He purportedly had ties to the Chicago Outfit and, in the late 1930s, to the New York-based Genovese crime family. The Minneapolis liquor underworld was run by Blumenfield's "combination," which continued controlling the liquor industry even after the prohibition of liquor was repealed in 1933.

In 1929, *Plain Talk* magazine, based in New York, declared Minneapolis one of the wettest states in the country. Its reporter alleged the existence of around 3,000 speakeasies and beer flats in Minneapolis and about 250 houses of prostitution with at least 5,000 professional prostitutes. Graft was paid to and collected by the Minneapolis Police Department with a local newspaperman estimating that 80 percent of the force was accepting illegal payments in one form or another. *Plain Talk* pegged the police force as "utterly demoralized." The moral stature of Minneapolis' law enforcement in 1929 was considered even lower than during the days of the Albert 'Doc" Ames mayoral administrations decades earlier.

Murder

Despite the number of crimes listed on his police record, Blumenfield spent little time in prison. He was believed responsible, though, for a number of killings, including that of a police officer. However, the most newsworthy murder occurred in 1935 when he was indicted for gunning down newspaper editor Walter Liggett. The journalist was killed in front

The alley in which Walter Liggett was murdered, at 1825 Second Avenue South in Minneapolis.

of his wife and 10-year-old daughter in the alley of his Minneapolis apartment building while unloading groceries.

At the time of the slaying, 34-year-old Blumenfield lived at 1525 Plymouth North and worked as a sales manager for Meyer Schuldberg at Chesapeake Brands Liquor, 115 Fifth Street Northeast in Minneapolis. Blumenfield swore that at the time of the killing, he was at the Artistic Barbershop on Hennepin Avenue between Fifth and Sixth Streets getting a shave, having his spats cleaned, shoes shined, and enjoying a tonic. He had a string of witnesses lined up to prove it.

According to a statement taken by Minneapolis Police Department Detective Kramer with Blumenfields's attorney, Charles Bank, present, Blumenfield admitted at 9 p.m. the night of the murder that he knew Liggett. He met the editor once by chance four weeks earlier in room 1013 at the Radisson Hotel in Minneapolis where his friend, Annette Fawcett, editor of the *Eye Opener* magazine, and former wife of publishing magnate "Captain Billy Fawcett lived, Blumenfield said. Fawcett had phoned Blumenfield asking him to come and meet the writer. Liggett had been running unflattering exposés on Blumenfield in his newspaper, the *Midwest American*. Blumenfield told police that Liggett was drunk that night and they argued.

When they were introduced, according to Blumenfield, Liggett took his measure and said, "So you are Kid Cann," and inquired about his relationship with Governor Floyd B. Olson and Hennepin County Attorney Ed Goff. Blumenfield said Liggett threatened him, stating that by the time he was through reporting on him, he would have Blumenfield and Olson sleeping in the same bed.

Blumenfield arrived at Fawcett's hotel room, he explained, to ask Liggett why he publicly railed against him, claiming to now be on the other side of the fence and to be legit. He told Liggett to leave him alone. He claimed Liggett said, "You are one of those smart Jews," and then made a pass at him. Blumenfield said he pushed the six-foot, four-inch Liggett, who fell, breaking a table leg.

Liggett reportedly started asking him for money for an upcoming trial and promised he would lay off writing about him for $1,500. He then asked Blumenfield to take him home. Blumenfield said he did not want to take Liggett home, but the editor insisted and Blumenfield relented. They left the hotel together and walked to Fifth Street where his car was parked. Fawcett's secretary, Felix Doran, who had accompanied the two, got into the car with them.

Blumenfield's story continued. Liggett insisted on stopping and getting another drink, but Blumenfield advised Liggett to go home. Still, the trio stopped at the Tia Juana Café where Blumenfield claimed he lost track of Liggett who disappeared outside. Only later did Blumenfield purportedly hear of a severe beating Liggett endured that night. He hadn't seen, or heard from, Liggett since that evening.

Fawcett told police that the day after Liggett's murder a few weeks later, Kid Cann called her office. She dodged his calls because "The sweetie she is going with now didn't want her to be going with Kid Cann." When interviewed by police on December 24, 1935, she told them that, to her, the shooting looked like a professional job. She also mentioned Charlie Ward, a big shot at the Brown & Bigelow company, whom Liggett had written about in his paper. She didn't think, though, that he had anything to do with the killing. Still, he had befriended many ex-convicts who might take it upon themselves to do the job for him.

Fawcett went missing, along with her secretary, Doran, at the onset of Kid Cann's trial. She was eventually located in Chicago, claiming she had been ready to appear at any time, but was not called.

Liggett's Version

This account of the meeting between Blumenfield and Liggett does not square with the account included in the book, *Stopping the Presses*, by Liggett's daughter, Marda, who witnessed his death. Liggett's wife, Edith, had received a number of phone calls at the office of the *Midwest American* from Fawcett, asking to speak to Liggett. She eventually left her number for him on Wednesday, October 25. When Liggett returned her call, Fawcett said she had information regarding a lawsuit in which Liggett was currently embroiled.

When Liggett arrived at the Radisson, he and Fawcett discussed the fact that he needed an attorney. Liggett admitted he had no way to raise the $1,500 to hire representation. She suggested that she could secure counseling for him at no cost, but he declined her offer. He didn't trust the firm. Fawcett then received a phone call and he overheard her tell the caller, "The gentleman is here now." She told Liggett it was Blumenfield on the line and asked Liggett if he wanted to talk to him. Liggett declined, stating he had nothing to say to him then, or any time.

Two men arrived while Fawcett was on the phone. One was Fawcett's secretary, Felix Doran, and the other was a Democratic politician. Liggett discussed current affairs with the politician who eventually left. Blumenfield arrived around 11 p.m. According to Edith Liggett, Blumenfield asked Liggett why he was writing derogatory things about him. The journalist replied that it was nothing personal. He was simply tired of seeing Minneapolis run by a gang of crooks and intended to expose Governor Olson's ties to the syndicate.

Blumenfield suggested that the *Midwest American* lay off or Liggett would be taken care of. Liggett also told him he didn't accept bribes and, if he did, he would be no better than the racketeers. Blumenfield swung at Liggett, who dodged the blow and then grabbed Blumenfield by the elbows and set him in a chair. He then announced he was leaving. Blumenfield apologized profusely and offered Liggett a ride – which

Liggett foolishly accepted. Blumenfield suggested they should have one more drink together and make up.

According to Edith Liggett, her husband, Blumenfield and Doran stopped at a bar on upper Hennepin Avenue where bootlegger Abe "Brownie" Brownstein was sitting at a table. Brownstein repeated the offer of a bribe and Liggett once again turned it down. He was attacked by Brownstein and Blumenfield but, being a trained boxer and in good shape, made his way outside to try and hail a cab. A group of men jumped from the alley, beat and kicked Liggett until he was nearly unconscious. During the beating, Liggett thought he saw a policeman standing on the edge of the crowd watching. When the thrashing ended, the badly injured Liggett found his way home in a taxi cab. His wife called for an ambulance, but was told three times that one was unavailable. After almost two hours, an ambulance arrived and took Liggett to Swedish Hospital at 914 South Eighth Street in Minneapolis.

Police and newspaper reports were unsympathetic to Liggett who was portrayed as a drunken brawler in police reports. An October 7 newspaper article stated that while in the Tia Juana Café at 1110 Hennepin Avenue, Liggett "became annoying to several customers by offering to display his pugilistic prowess." Liggett reportedly "tussled" with Abe Brownstein, breaking Brownstein's thumb. Brownstein admitted to striking Liggett once after his thumb was broken. No charges were filed and the police absolved Blumenfield and Fawcett of any part in the assault. In the end, Liggett eventually healed from his injuries and won his court case, representing himself.

The victory was short-lived and, as promised, Liggett was "taken care of" with five shots to the heart. Blumenfield was indicted for Liggett's murder weeks later. But after a lengthy trial, and even with positive identifications by Liggett's wife and a neighbor's boyfriend, Blumenfield was acquitted.

Liquor Industry Owned by Kid Cann

During Prohibition, FBI files show Blumenfield worked in conjunction with Minneapolis' Ed "Barney" Berman and Abe "Brownie" Brownstein, considered by the FBI to be the largest alcohol peddlers in the nation. In addition to owning local liquor establishments, the "combination" eventually held extensive real estate interests in Minneapolis and Miami Beach, Florida. They also owned an interest in the El Cortez Hotel and Gambling Casino in Las Vegas, Nevada. Mobster Moe Sedway owned the other half of the casino which they sold in 1945. Though the group had connections with Davie "The Jew" Berman and Charles "Chickie" Berman, in 1946 Brownstein told investigators they no longer worked with the Berman brothers as they were "old school" and considered themselves "strong arm men."

After Prohibition was repealed in 1933, the "combination" continued to run the Minneapolis liquor industry. According to Minneapolis FBI file 33-35A-17:

> ISADORE BLUMENFIELD, wa. Kid Cann, heads the liquor group in Minneapolis and controls the issuances of all liquor licenses in the city of Minneapolis, for which he and his group get from $5,000 - $20,000. ISADORE BLUMENFIELD wa. Kid Cann, and his Jewish associates are known as the "combination" and control most of the liquor places in Minneapolis. He (name redacted) said that it was his understanding that THOMAS W. BANKS and the "combination" control 70% of all legitimate liquor places in Minneapolis. He remarked that the "combination" controls liquor matters only and "the syndicate" controls gambling and slot machines. He said that KID CANN is the alleged head of the "combination" and that THOMAS W. BANKS, according to his sources, is a big shot in both "the syndicate" and the "combination."

The Blumenfield gang held multiple liquor licenses throughout Minneapolis and ran the Chicago-Franklin liquor store at 800 Franklin Avenue, the East Side liquor store at 429 East Hennepin Avenue, the Lake Street liquor store at 9 East Lake Street, Harold's at 900 Marquette Avenue and the Loring Liquor Store at 1370 Nicollet Avenue. Blumenfield's relatives also owned Danny's at 1416 Chicago Avenue and the Flame Bar at 1523 Nicollet Avenue. But the heat was on and local authorities were cracking down on licensing issues.

Blumenfield and his wife, Lillian, had no children, so doted on their relatives. He put one nephew through medical school and helped another, a WW II veteran, start Café 1400. Upset with ongoing press coverage, Blumfield complained:

> "Every time the papers print something about 'Kid Cann,' it hurts them children," he said. "They have to suffer because some politician is trying to make headlines.'

  He publicly defended himself against charges of manipulating liquor licenses in Minneapolis, then announced he was "kissing off" Minneapolis and moving to Miami, Florida. The Blumenfields left behind their home at 2305 Mount View Avenue and another house, which they'd never moved into, at 5900 Oakland Avenue.
  The couple moved to Miami Beach, settling into the Executive House, a new, upscale oceanfront apartment building owned by Ben Cohen, former attorney for Miami's gambling syndicate. Blumenfield's brother, Yiddy, joined him there to manage their real estate interests. Blumenfield also reportedly held real estate interests with Cleveland bootlegger-gambler Thomas J. McGinty and associates of Meyer Lansky, one of the founders of the "National Crime Syndicate" in the United States. Blumenfield hoped his family in Minneapolis could live in peace once he'd left the city. He told a reporter in an interview that he and his wife had plenty of money to get by on and that he had no need to make any deals for the rest of his life. Many individuals in the city doubted he was letting go of Minneapolis altogether.
  Eventually, publicity generated by the Congressional Kefauver Crime Committee report published in August 1951 prompted the sale of the "combination's" Miami property. It was one of the largest Florida real estate deals around that time.
  An article in *Colliers* magazine dated September 29, 1951, called Isadore Blumenfield, wa. Kid Cann, one of the most powerfully entrenched gangsters in gangster-ridden Miami Beach. The writer accused Jules Beeman, a partner in Miami's "little syndicate," of running an illegal gambling concession at Blumenfield's Martinique Hotel.
  Blumenfield resented the accusation of operating illegal businesses, explaining that his income came from stocks and bonds in companies like Sears & Roebuck, Montgomery Ward and Seagram's Distilleries Companies. He argued that those companies weren't targeted as run by

gangsters and racketeers just because he owned stock in them.

He was clearly sore at implications cast upon a specific investment in Twin City Rapid Transit Company. Blumenfield told a local reporter that he and his wife bought stocks as a favor to some people, never actually admitting the identity of those individuals. The Transit Company stock, he emphasized, was disposed of as quickly as purchased, causing the couple to lose money. He complained that he could have selected better stock by closing his eyes and punching a pin into the stock listed in the *Minneapolis Tribune* business section.

Leonard E. Lindquist, a member of the Minnesota Railroad and Warehouse Commission, accused the Twin City Rapid Transit Company of being under the influence of racketeers after a jury found Fred A. Ossanna, Benson M. Larrick and Harry H. Isaacs guilty of mail and wire fraud violations, transporting property fraudulently obtained in interstate commerce, and of a conspiracy to commit offenses against the United States for disposing of surplus steel and cars.

Said Blumenfield:

> "That Lindquist (a member of the state railroad and warehouse commission) talks about racketeers in a town where there aren't any rackets. He's just trying to blow himself up for governor or something."

Osanna, then general counsel for the company, led the stockholder charge to replace the TCRT's president, Charles Green, whom he accused of causing strife. He replaced Green as president.

Under Osanna's administration, the transit system was hastily changed from running streetcars to populating the streets with buses. As a result, there was a sudden inventory of salvage from tracks and cars. The problems began with the disposition of this salvage.

In 1959, Blumenfield was indicted by a federal grand jury as a co-conspirator in a million dollar fraud against the Twin City Rapid Transit Company. True to form, he was again acquitted.

His luck ran out in 1960, however, when he and fellow white slave transporter Monte Perkins were found guilty by a jury of twelve men in a case involving a young woman. Marilyn Ann Tollefson had been transported across state lines for immoral purposes. Then, in 1961, he was convicted of trying to bribe a juror during a liquor syndicate trial. Blumenfield served a federal prison term for the convictions.

Twin City Rapid Transit Company burning out-of-date streetcars.
Photo courtesy of the Hennepin County Library.

First They Negotiate

Local Twin City historian Bob Patrin believes his uncle, a small business owner, was the victim of Kid Cann's mob. After being discharged from the U.S. Army in 1944, Patrin's uncle, Frank Fietek, leased a piece of property called "Swing City" just outside St. Paul city limits. The building was originally a garage owned by H. S. Quatman at 1682 Rice Street; he had expanded it to include a bar, but lost his license for serving liquor to minors. Through the help of his veterans' benefits, Fietek and his sister-in-law, Marie, opened the business of his dreams. Meanwhile, across Rice Street, which now divides Maplewood and Roseville, sat the Happy Hollow, frequented by organized crime member Tommy Banks.

Securing a liquor license in 1944 wasn't easy, with most having been claimed by Kid Cann's combination. But Ramsey County managed to locate one for Fietek that had just expired.

Patrin was fourteen and a collector of license plates when he visited the property with his uncle for the first time. He got his uncle's permission to dig around in the garage for license plates. Patrin climbed several steps and entered through a door he believed would take him to the garage. But, instead, he found himself in a space with what appeared to be dressing rooms scattered with discarded women's clothing. Each cubicle had a black curtain partitioning it from the main part of the room. Patrin had stumbled into an abandoned den of white slavery where men paid to have intimate relations with women. On a bentwood chair lay a sap, often referred to as a "blackjack," and used to beat people. The property had been abandoned hastily and the goods left behind moved to his grandfather's garage.

Fietek purchased the property, renamed it Frank and Marie's Tavern, and ran it as a family restaurant and dance hall. About 1 ½ months after the business opened, Fietek was visited by two bagmen, representatives of a local crime organization. They suggested to Fietek that he might need a partner. Each man pulled a roll of bills from his pocket, depositing $2000 on the table in front of him.

"I've already got a partner. My Uncle Sam," Fietek informed them. He declined their offer and did not expect to see them again. But they returned a few weeks later, this time pointing out that his business was outside of city limits. Law enforcement, they emphasized, would not cross the street to help him if there was trouble. He was outside of Minneapolis, Sheriff Tommy Gibbons' jurisdiction.

Frank Fietek in front of Frank and Marie's, 1945.
Photo courtesy of Bob Patrin.

Fietek loved his new business and took out a large ad in the Hudson Map book to promote it. Frank and Marie's had not seen any trouble until the bagmen came around. Shortly after Fietek turned down their offer for a partner, fights began breaking out at Frank and Marie's, leaving blood on their dance floor. The bagmen providentially came around again, offering protection against fights and riots. A worried neighbor watched as a long black Lincoln, easily recognized as a car owned by the mob and bearing passengers who resembled local Jewish organized crime members, turned the corner and parked in front of Marie's house. The men got out and went to the door with a gift, a $75 purse. It was an incentive for Fietek to talk her brother-in-law into giving up their lease.

"What did those men want?" the neighbor, a Jewish attorney asked Marie after they left.

"They gave me this purse," she told him.

"Well give it back. Those guys are members of the mob."

"How can I give it back?" she asked, shaken. "You just said they're the mob. I can't very well give it back to them."

Marie shoved the purse onto a shelf in the back of her closet where it sat for several years until she gave it to her son who gifted it to a girl he was dating. Marie could not convince her brother-in-law to give up his lease and Fietek did not appear to understand, or was unwilling to believe, that he was dealing with organized crime. But Marie was shaken and had her name removed from the lease.

One evening Frank Fietek was closing up Frank and Marie's when the bagmen appeared and told him to get into their car. They were going for a ride. Frank got in and was driven into the country where the men beat him with a leaded bat, breaking both of his legs and leaving him in agony and in an extremely dangerous position in the middle of County Road D north of St. Paul. At the time, the speed limit was 35 miles an hour and the consequence of speeding would have been the loss of two months of gas rationing. So drivers were careful to follow the law. This moderate speed gave the driver who found Fietek the chance to miss running him over. The driver got Fietek into the car and drove him to Anchor Hospital in St. Paul. He survived, but was badly disabled. Upon his release from the hospital, he moved into a duplex owned by his brother. Fietek's brother and sister-in-law could assist him with household chores and care for him.

In the meantime, a fire started in the basement of Frank and Marie's Tavern, causing roughly $2,500 in damage to the property. When the lease came up for renewal in November of 1945, the business was no longer operating. Still, Fietek would not give up the lease.

"Tell everyone I'm renewing," Fietek told his family. "I'm not giving it up, even if I can't run it."

According to an article in the *St. Paul Dispatch*, Fietek took his own life in his home not long afterward. But those who knew the extent of Fietek's injuries believed his death was no suicide. Fietek was found in the basement of his duplex, hanging from the ceiling, with a pile of wood scattered under him, the official story states. He reportedly climbed onto the wood to hang himself. According to the police report, he had put on a necktie, then threaded a wire through it, wrapped the wire around a pipe in the ceiling and kicked the logs out from underneath himself. The extreme injuries to his legs suffered in the attack by the bagmen on lonely County Road D made the official story questionable.

His funeral was held at the St. Paul Cathedral with burial as an honored veteran in Fort Snelling National Cemetery. At the wake, the night before Fietek's funeral, a bagman showed up and talked to 15-year-old Patrin. It was apparently a code of honor among organized crime members to attend the wakes of those they had slain.

"It's too bad about your uncle," the bagman told Patrin, "but he was such a hard headed Polack. He must have been in so much pain – and then the chair slipped."

Patrin said the bagman seemed like a nice man at the time. He didn't learn the details of his uncle's death until later. Patrin has a small ad in his possession showing that, despite significant damage caused by the fire, Frank and Marie's was re-opened in a matter of weeks as the old Swing City – just as if nothing had ever happened and his uncle wasn't lying beneath a new mound of fresh dirt in the Fort Snelling National Cemetery

Frank Fietek's military funeral at Fort Snelling in March 1946. Photo courtesy of Bob Patrin.

Davie "The Jew" Berman

In her book, Easy Street, Susan Berman writes about her father, underworld figure Davie "The Jew" Berman, who moved to Minneapolis in 1934 at the age of thirty-one. Berman had just done time in Sing Sing Prison in New York for a post office robbery in Wisconsin. His brother, Charles "Chickie" Berman, was already running the book for the gambling industry in the Twin Cities.

Chickie Berman had been coached by his brother from prison, a benefit due to Berman's exemplary behavior, which won him a place with the warden's family on weekend visits. Berman did office work for Warden Lawes and had access to a phone. Via phone calls, Berman walked Chickie through opening the White Bear Lodge, a gambling establishment in St. Paul.

Berman was an acquaintance of mob boss Bugsy Siegel, founder of Murder Incorporated. Once free, Berman reconnected with the mobster. He was in good standing with the mob, having kept his mouth shut after his arrest for the post office robbery.

With New York Mayer Fiorella La Guardia waging war against mobster Frank Costello's racketeering and slot machines, the mob was looking for new ground. Berman was promoted to lieutenant by National Crime Syndicate leaders Meyer Lansky and Lucky Luciano. He was offered $1,000,000 for his loyalty, but turned it down with a request of his own:

> "All I want is something from your pocket. Money to get to Minneapolis. I'll pay it back when I can. And I want permission to run Minneapolis for you – just gambling."

With a nod, Minneapolis was given away. Gambling ran fairly uninterrupted by either Mayor Thomas Latimer from 1935–1939 or under Mayor George Leach's administration from 1939–1941.

The city's underworld was waiting for the arrival of Davie Berman, having heard a great deal about him. He arrived donning a dark suit and with his black hair slicked back, impressing with his connections to the underworld. His brother, Chickie, was thrilled to see him. Chickie and his partner, Ed Fried, immediately offered Berman a cut of their action. Berman quickly broadened the business, adding more clubs, a race wire, and slot and pinball machines. Berman's Jewish syndicate was on friendly terms with the Irish combination, but ran in rivalry with Kid Cann's organization.

During the 1940 Minneapolis mayoral election, Berman's group made large political donations to Mayor Marvin Kline's campaign. Once Kline was safely in office, Berman kicked Kid Cann's gambling enterprise out of Minneapolis and enjoyed a lucrative business relationship with the Kline administration. Berman worked hard to maintain a good relationship with the mob out East, often offering refuge to mobsters who were running from the law for murder charges. An FBI report called Davie Berman a "stick up man and killer." It went on to say that:

> "Both Dave and Chickie Berman, his brother, associate with Philip alias Flippy Scher, notorious Minneapolis killer who was recently discharged from the army and presently operates a gambling joint at 318 Nicollet, Minneapolis."

Berman had to constantly stay vigilant to protect Minneapolis from the Chicago Italians, particularly Al Capone's gang. Berman's daughter describes an evening when one of Capone's shills arrived at Berman's nightclub to advise him that Capone's boys were looking for him.

Berman said to the shill, "They're looking for me? Well, tell them I'm looking for them – tonight, and I won't need this." He pulled the gun from his chest holster and threw it on the table. Berman's men became alarmed. Chickie and the others warned Berman to be careful as he left the club. He was gone until the early morning hours, negotiating with Capone's men at his hotel room. Berman returned to the club bragging, "I told them to keep their greaseballs out of my town."

A message arrived from Capone the following day stating that he agreed to stay out of Minneapolis, but Berman had better stay out of

Chicago or he was dead.

Berman belonged to Minneapolis and was known as a "good racketeer." Berman's racing book was located at the Radisson hotel for six months, then for six months at the Dyckman Hotel. The crap and card game moved to new locations on a regular basis. Berman was known as a generous and kind man, handing out $100 bills to losing gamblers, hating to think of the men's families going hungry due to bad luck and vice.

According to Susan Berman, her father and her Uncle Chickie took the Midwest race wire, setting the gambling lines which were known as the best in the country. The Bermans also owned the pinball and jukebox business in Minneapolis. Golf caddie Rich Natz joined the business and was dispatched to small towns. There he dined with mayors and chiefs of police, suggesting that they weigh the possibility of opening gambling clubs in their towns. The propositions were sweetened with bribes.

Natz wasn't allowed to gamble in Berman's parlors and was given the task of watching Chickie, who had a propensity for losing a great deal of money at his own tables. Chickie would have Natz hold his fat roll of cash for him, peeling off $100 bills at a time to bet until the roll was gone. Chickie occasionally found himself in hot water with the mob for not paying his markers. He was saved only by being Davie Berman's brother.

The Dyckman Hotel where Dave Berman ran his bookmaking operation. Photo courtesy of the Hennepin County Library.

As a Minneapolis resident, Davie Berman was not considered classy enough to join the Jewish golf clubs. But he dined regularly with doctors, lawyers and politicians at Manny's Steak House in Minneapolis. He didn't smoke, drink or swear in front of women and swore he would only marry a virgin – which he did when he married Gladys Evans (born Elizabeth Lynell Ewald), a resident of St. Paul. She performed with her cousin as a dancer on stages in Minneapolis. Berman met and became smitten with the beautiful young woman sixteen years his junior. On November 29, 1939, the two tied the knot.

Two years later, in 1941, rejected by the United States military because of his criminal background, Berman headed north to Canada and joined the 18th Armored Car Regiment of the 12th Manitoba Dragoons.

Chickie Berman enlisted in the United States Army and served until he was injured by a land mine in 1943. When Berman returned to Minneapolis in 1944, recovering from those serious wounds, he found the town no longer wide open. Hubert Humphrey was running for mayor with promises to clean up the city. Humphrey struck a deal with Berman's group, agreeing he wouldn't arrest or make a spectacle out of them if they quietly left town.

Davie Berman received permission from national crime syndicate leader, Meyer Lansky. to move out West. He got in touch with Bugsy Siegel with plans to relocate to Las Vegas.

Chickie Berman borrowed money from the gambling "combination" and bought The Stockholm restaurant in White Bear Lake. His brother helped run the business while closing down his own clubs. Davie Berman also got a suitcase of $1,000,000 together for purchase of the El Cortez Hotel in Las Vegas. Chickie was gambling heavily and Berman worried about covering his brother's losses. It was too dangerous for Chickie to stay in Minneapolis, so Berman took him along out West with his young wife and new baby, Susan.

The Disappearance of Anthony DeVito

In 1958, Minnesota resident Alex DeGood was serving time in the South Carolina State Penitentiary for burglary. While there, he spilled the beans to Law Enforcement Division Chief J.P. Strom about the murder of 24-year-old Anthony DeVito of St. Paul. DeGood had been arrested during the summer of 1953 for a $400 robbery at the Huggins store in Aynor, South Carolina. He was transported to Charleston for prosecution along with Minnesotans Rocky Lupino, John Azzone, Anthony DeVito and Fred William Mussehl.

DeVito and Mussehl confessed to their parts in the crime and were released on bond pending their trials. Both men returned to Minnesota. All but DeVito, who was expected to be a state's witness, returned to South Carolina as the trial date neared. DeGood made the astonishing claim that he had accompanied Lupino in the kidnapping of DeVito. He revealed that DeVito was murdered to prevent him from testifying. DeVito was buried east of St Paul, although his body was never found.

Lupino and Azzone were arrested in South Carolina under the Fugitive Felon Act and held on $100,000 bond for the murder of DeVito. The men were found guilty of kidnapping and were sent to prison in 1958. They could not be found guilty of murder without DeVito's body as evidence.

Rocky Lupino and the "Dago" Gang

Rocco Salvatore Lupino was born November 4, 1916, to a poor family in Dog Town, an Italian neighborhood in northeast Minneapolis. As a youth, he took part in territorial gang fights where East Hennepin Avenue divided the northeast and southeast Minneapolis clans. Street fights had rules of honor during the Depression that called for no weapons to be used. Individuals sporting guns or knives were considered "crazies."

Lupino was first arrested at age 22 in 1938 on burglary charges. Only years later was he rumored to be connected to organized crime. Police files describe him as 5'8 ½", 182 lbs, with black hair, maroon eyes, a dark complexion and a muscular build. His occupation is listed as bartender, his residence as 418 Johnson Street in northeast Minneapolis. As the years go by, police records and photographs document the aging of the criminal with his hair going from black to bald and his build changing from muscular to husky.

By the 1940s, the Minneapolis Police Department labeled Lupino, who had an extensive criminal record, as the city's number one police problem. Although he was a criminal at an early age, Lupino was good to his parents and, later, to his wife and children. His wife, Mae, said that people often asked why she never left him. She told them her children adored their father and that he spoiled them. He was a good provider. He sent her flowers for birthdays and anniversaries, even when he served time in prison. Though he never told her where he was when he was not home, when he was home, he was gentle and quiet.

On June 3, 1953, a letter was sent by Bureau of Criminal Apprehension Superintendent John J. Tierney to the sheriff in Barron, Wisconsin, bearing the names of the men he called "The Dago Gang." They included Lupino, Sandy Roy Scavo, John Frank Azzone, Edward Joseph Capra, Louis William Lepora, and John Frank Mancino.

In 1958, Lupino was sentenced to eighty years in Stillwater Prison for the 1953 kidnapping of 24-year-old Anthony Ralph DeVito. He was released on parole on February 17, 1971. His parole was revoked on September 21, 1972, when he was arrested in a north Minneapolis residence for illegal possession of a firearm. He also served a five-year term in Alcatraz Federal Penitentiary. after fleeing Minnesota to avoid prosecution. Lupino was paroled in 1979 and returned to northeast Minneapolis to live with his sister. In 1980, he was sought for gambling violations and the slaying of jeweler Giovanni Maccaddino of Skokie, Illinois.

According to the book, *Minneapolis Organized Crime* by Knute Bidem, when Lupino was finally freed from prison, he planned to get back in the rackets. But things had changed. He wanted to act as bookie and run the entire five-state area, with the exception of Milwaukee and Madison, and he wanted to start immediately. Unfortunately for Lupino, Kid Cann was no longer the Godfather of Minneapolis and the new Capra / Patterson syndicate had a different approach to business. He was invited to the Campus Pizza Restaurant by his old friend Jack Capra who offered him a job as a gambling debt collector. Lupino refused and they reportedly parted on unfriendly terms.

Lupino and his good friend "Smolak the Polak," a petty criminal from northeast Minneapolis, got jobs at the Berman Buckskin Company in Minneapolis in order to pull down a big score. At closing time, Smolak hid in an office and Lupino brought a truck back to the factory. Once there, they loaded up $100,000 worth of merchandise at midnight. In the morning, Smolak showed up for work wearing one of the stolen coats and police were alerted. But they could not prove he was in on the crime. Just the same, he was fired. Lupino sold the goods and kept the profits for himself.

In February of 1982, local newspapers reported that Rocky Lupino, career criminal from northeast Minneapolis, died in a jail in Springfield, Missouri, hanging from the business end of a strip of prison sheet strung over a showerhead. His feet barely skimmed a stack of books on the floor. Though the official story reported Lupino's death a suicide, those who knew him realized his hands were weakened by arthritis or a degenerative disease for which he had been treated at the Mayo Clinic in Rochester. It was unlikely he could have torn the sheet into strips or knotted it tightly. He was facing extradition charges to Indiana on a murder charge at the time of his stay.

Call the Coroner

The details are sketchy, but, according to a local retired police officer, during the 1920's, the Wright County Coroner was on occasion summoned to treat the wounds that organized crime members sustained during gun fights. The old coroner, who was referred to as "Doc" claimed he was picked up in a long black Cadillac at night by two men in suits and told to "bring your bag and don't ask any questions." The mobsters would then drive him to a secluded lake. Once there, the men would flash their car lights twice and a boat would come and ferry them out to an island.

The criminals chose an island to work from, so they wouldn't have to worry about surprise attacks. Once he was finished sewing up his patient, the coroner would be driven home and paid five dollars in gold pieces for his time. The coroner was warned never to say a word, and was frightened every time he was called upon to provide medical services. It only happened a few times, according to Doc, but he could brag that he never lost a patient.

CHAPTER 10
BIRTH OF THE BALDIES

Small World

Funny story. While attending a meeting in Bloomington, I mentioned that I was writing a book and was just learning about the Baldies, a 1960s street gang.

"I was a Baldy."

"You were?" I looked closer at George, who's in his seventies. He told me about growing up near Deuce Casper and how quickly Deuce's mood could change from friendly to dangerous. I filed this information away, just in case.

Now, fast forward to the pizza place where I was meeting Mr. X. I told him about the guy in Bloomington who claimed to be a Baldy. Mr. X looked at me for a moment, then set his slice of pizza on his plate.

"A lot of guys say they were Baldies, but they weren't," Mr. X remarked, wiping his hands on a greasy paper napkin. "What's his name?"

"George."

"George who?"

"I don't know," I answered, feeling a little stupid, though I have known

George on a first-name basis for years. "But he said he was friends with Deuce Casper and that Casper couldn't be trusted."

That was good enough for Mr. X. He asked me to find out if George's last name was McQuistin. Apparently George had icon status in the Baldy movement.

A phone call later, I confirmed that I was, indeed, friends with a real member of the legendary Baldies. The down side—I couldn't divulge Mr. X's identity to George. But he didn't press. George commented that he'd recently seen fellow Baldy, Tommy Ogdahl who held a certain stature in the city.

I can't help thinking that this is truly a small, small world. And isn't it odd that a simple farm girl from southwestern Minnesota should know these dubious men?

Elizabeth Johanneck

Hub of Hell

There exists within the city of Minneapolis, at the corner of 26th Street and 26th Avenue, a location referred to by Mr. X, and others, as "The Hub of Hell." In the 1960s, the area housed saloons, nightclubs, strip joints and a bowling alley where corrupt cops could strike bargains with the city's underworld.

Within this underbelly of Minneapolis lurked gang members known as the Baldies. They had street names like James "Deuce" Casper, Perry "The Scholar" Millik, and Tommy "The Bomber" Ogdahl. The youths fought their battles there and, in some cases, crossed the line into organized crime.

Steel workers from the Minneapolis Moline factory joined young men and women coming of age during the era of the Vietnam War. Needing to work off a little excess energy, these youth sometimes participated in gangland fights behind places like Duffy's Bar, Pearson's, the Hexagon, Nibs and the Stardust bowling alley, much to the delight of onlookers. These unnecessary battles kept the old General Hospital emergency room hopping on weekends.

The ranks of the Baldies grew exponentially. They were a mean lot whose main interest was to feel knuckles smashing against flesh and bone. They attacked innocent bystanders in cold blood, leaving their victims badly hurt, humiliated and confused. These were troubled times.

In the book, *Tommy (The Bomber) Ogdahl and the Baldies*, E. J. Johnson documents former Minneapolis Deputy Mayor and Alderman Ogdahl's fights as a Baldy. The "Bomber" earned his nickname as a little guy who packed a wallop, knocking his opponents out with just one blow. His fist was "the bomb." The biography estimates that Ogdahl was involved in over seven hundred street fights, losing only a couple.

Ogdahl's book records his first six-month stint in a reform school, the Hennepin County Home School (aka Glen Lake School for Boys), in Minnetonka at the age of thirteen. "The Bomber" found himself recommitted for an additional six months for fighting. He was no stranger to jail and the workhouse.

Ogdahl was a model Baldy, detailed in his published description of the anatomy of a fight. A fight, he explains in Johnson's book, comprised the recognition, or making, of an enemy; the agreement to fight; the negotiation of place and time; and the bloody details of the battle. He disputes the suggestion of race wars between young blacks and whites during the 1960s. A fight was a fight. Color of the opponent didn't matter. Ogdahl also describes the toll drugs took on young men and women when this new form of contraband rolled onto the black market.

Ogdahl changed his stripes as he grew up, eventually getting elected Minneapolis alderman for the 8th ward and as deputy mayor, serving under Mayor Charles Stenvig. Ogdahl was rumored, however, to have had close ties with International Brotherhood of Teamsters Union President Jimmy Hoffa Jr.

On May 19, 1961, the *New York Times* carried an article headlined Social Workers Etch Dilemma: To Help Youths or Aid Police, which reported a meeting of the National Conference of Social Welfare in Minneapolis. The purpose of the meeting debated the dilemma posed to social workers when working with youth street gangs. Should social workers be allowed to withhold information given to them by the youngster or should they report it to the police department? Conference attendees saw trust as absolutely necessary in working with disaffected youths, but were concerned that social workers often obtained information best shared with law enforcement.

"Perhaps," suggested Russell Hogrefe, executive director of Chicago Youth Centers, "a possible solution would be legal sanction for privileged communications similar to that granted doctors, lawyers and ministers."

A year later local newspapers reported a meeting of police chiefs from Minneapolis, St. Paul and the surrounding suburbs to discuss the growing problem of violence between two rival gangs, the Animals and the Baldies. The article described the Animals as a high school gang founded around 1960 and hailing from the north and northeast suburban Minneapolis area. Their rivals, the Baldies, were concentrated in south Minneapolis and associated only with members of their group. The Baldies reportedly inflicted injury upon their victims by mercilessly kicking them with heavy shoes.

Despite Mayor Hubert Humphrey's routing of the most notorious gangsters from Minneapolis a decade earlier, a new criminal element had been born.

Minneapolis Police Captain Ray Williamson, head of the juvenile division, advised that not all youth with short hair and dressed like Baldies were gang members.

In contrast to members of the Animals who dressed casually in blue jeans, the Baldies' dress code called for wardrobes which couldn't be purchased in run-of-the-mill mercantiles like J.C. Penney. Rather, their clothing came from Dayton's, Liemondt's and Rothchilds in Minneapolis or from Peck & Peck and Brooks Brothers in Chicago. Specifics required Gant shirts, Corbin slacks and wing tip shoes with shell cordovans from Florscheim. Pendelton shirts were allowed, though, along with Dobbs hats, and alligator belts. Shirts needed a bar collar and cuff links. Knee high socks were held up with garters. If tennis shoes were worn, they had to be low cut Keds with a blue stripe. Outer wear included loden and teddy bear coats, camel or herringbone dress coats, or hero jackets. In the summertime, khaki pants were worn with gray t-shirts, a straw hat, and sunglasses. In contrast to today's trend where "gangstas" wear their pants hanging low, the crotches of Baldies' pants needed to be high enough to avoid tripping when attempting to kick someone in the head.

According to the book, *Minneapolis Organized Crime 1900 - 2000* by Knute Bidem, if you did not have a close friend who knew Baldy founder Deuce Casper, were not trained as a criminal, or had not done time in an institution, you were not a Baldy. If you could not dress properly or fend for yourself in the inner city, you were not a Baldy. Period.

James "Deuce" Casper (1936 – 2003)

The young man credited with founding the Baldies was the mercurial James "Deuce" Casper, born in 1936 in south Minneapolis. He was raised in the Philips neighborhood, across the street from the cop-killing O'Kasick brothers, two of whom lost their lives in a 1957 shootout with police in the Carlos Avery Game Preserve in Anoka. A third O'Kasick brother survived the shootout and later committed suicide in the Minnesota State Reformatory in St. Cloud.

Casper was nicknamed "Deuce," the low end of a deck of cards, after his brother, "Ace" Casper, five years his senior. Their mother struggled to raise the pair when their father, a teamster, died at a young age. Ace mentored his younger brother and, as a means of discipline, delivered powerful blows to Deuce's head that sometimes dropped the boy to the floor.

In 1955, Deuce Casper and his best friend, Al Brown, began organizing the toughest students in south Minneapolis in to the antithesis of their rivals, the Animals. Instead of combing their greased hair into ducktails and donning leather jackets, the Baldies emulated gangster Kid Cann's meticulous style. They wore closely cropped hair and expensive clothing like the male models in Esquire and Gentlemen's Quarterly.

At six-feet, three inches, Casper presented an imposing figure—big, mean, and agile. His meaty hands could deal a ringing blow. Teen-aged boys hanging out at Emil's Pool Hall and Bar on Nicollet and Lake Streets would stop shooting pool and talking smart when Deuce Casper strolled in. They would stand in deferential silence knowing, but not acknowledging, his identity. Over a ten-year period, roughly one thousand Baldies were initiated by the Casper machine to instill fear and wreak havoc across Minneapolis.

The Baldies and their gang rivals, the Animals, were arch enemies. Jacque Simon, the most feared brawler in northeast Minneapolis, led the Animals. Local folklore holds that Casper knocked Simon out with a single kick to the head then continued to beat him up every time he saw him for about ten years. Casper is remembered, too, for knocking out a new-car salesman at the Grossman Chevrolet car lot. He was also jailed for five years in 1957 for beating up Minneapolis Police Officer Gustafson, who patrolled the Lake Street area.

The United States Army accepted Casper with a waiver for his criminal activity. Upon his release for assaulting Gustafson, he lost the opportunity to serve after committing a minor infraction that put him in the workhouse. His chances of playing professional hockey, for which he'd been offered scholarships, were now behind him.

Within a short time of being released from jail, he was once again behind bars at Stillwater State Prison in southeastern Minnesota on a forgery offense. When not in prison or a reform school, Casper worked intermittently as a bouncer in bars owned by the overlord of the Minneapolis underworld, Kid Cann. Casper ran errands for Cann's alleged hit men, John Azzone and Rocky Lupino.

Between prison stays, Casper was also a brawler and a jewel and armed car thief. He spent half his adult life in workhouses and prisons among Mafia dons, murderers and fellow Baldies. He did time in correctional facilities in St. Cloud and Stillwater, Minnesota; Lompoc, Folsum, and San Quentin in California; Lewisburg, Pennsylvania; and Leavenworth, Kansas.

He died in 2003, never fully recovering from open heart surgery.

Perry "The Scholar" Millik (1944 – 2003)

Perry Millik was the son of a Nazi soldier who died defending Berlin in 1945. His mother was an interpreter for the German Air Force and fluent in five languages. After World War II, she migrated with her small son to south Minneapolis where they lived in poverty with relatives.

In a battle to escape grueling hardship, Millik scavenged his neighborhood for odd jobs. While still in grade school, he formed a street gang of eight boys who ran a significant shoplifting and fencing operation. By the time he was in junior high school, Millik had become a major Minneapolis drug dealer.

Considered an accomplished fighter, Millik was sent to reform school after attempting an extremely violent robbery. Yet he managed to graduate from high school with honors. This was no small feat given he was running a commercial burglary ring at night. Millik was committed to the Minneapolis Workhouse immediately after high school. After doing his stretch, he joined the United States Army, served proudly and was honorably discharged.

He then entered college, earning two degrees. In an ironic twist, Millik accepted a position with the corrections department. He might have stayed on the right path if not for the release of Deuce Casper from prison. The two decided there was more money in crime than legitimate commerce, so Millik put his brilliant mind to work devising ways to beat the system. He eventually owned over one hundred buildings in the Twin Cities area and engaged in massive real estate fraud and drug manufacturing houses. Millik also acted as the front man for the Lebanese Alexander Brothers who sent a cut of their porn and prostitution profits to the old Genovese crime family in New York.

Married with two children, Millik was intellectual, and authored *5000*

Years of Graffitti, Philosphy, and Humor.

According to the book *Minneapolis Organized Crime 1900-2000* by Knute Bidem, Millik and Casper, despite liking Minnesota Senator Paul Wellstone, once pulled a heist on Wellstone's campaign. They stole a barrel full of donations, then separated the cash from the checks and personally delivered the latter to Wellstone in person.

Millik died in 2003 under mysterious circumstances and, according to Minneapolis Organized Crime, his ashes were scattered from atop the Foshay Tower in downtown Minneapolis.

Jack "The Book" Capra

Jack Capra, along with his business partner, George Patterson, took over the control of all illegal gambling throughout the upper Midwest from Minneapolis gangster Kid Cann, according to Minneapolis Organized Crime 1900 – 2000. They also oversaw other forms of criminal activity and operated under the auspices of the old Genovese mafia family from New York City.

Tut Tilseth

Tut Tilseth became a close friend of Perry Millik when Tilseth was placed in a foster home in Minneapolis. Though not Millik's intellectual equal, he had a wild side and ties to the Baldies. That intrigued Millik and the two became close friends. Tilseth, however, appeared to lack any sense of loyalty. In an effort to bolster his reputation, Tilseth challenged Millik to a fight, asserting, "Perry, I really like you, but I need to know if I can kick your ass."

Millik reportedly responded, "That's fine, but this means I'll have to hospitalize you." Millik was enraged by Tilseth's challenge. However he told Tilseth, "...we can still be friends."

The fight was scheduled for the following Friday behind Phil's Drugstore on 35th and 4th Avenue, so that it could be witnessed by members of the Baldies and other curious adolescents. Before the designated date, Millik was caught in a brutal brawl with another youth, Jack Conner, and nearly beat him in to a coma. Having caught wind of the fight, Tilseth tried to back out, but Millik wouldn't allow it. Tilseth was saved from what could have been a deadly beating by being arrested and sent to the Red Wing Reform School just prior to the designated event.

Tilseth later paid his dues when a dental student at the University of Minnesota, who had suffered from Tilseth's bullying, purposely injected Novocain into the wrong tooth. Tilseth writhed in pain as the student extracted, and then pocketed, a rotten molar. Years later, upon news of Tilseth's death, it is rumored the dentist, out of respect, took the tooth outside and buried it.

George McQuistin

George McQuistin, whose name appears in the biography of Tommy Ogdahl, was a self-described "hot-head." This quality made him a perfect candidate for gang membership. McQuistin grew up across the street from Baldies' leader, Deuce Casper, in south Minneapolis and knew him well.

McQuistin, in his 70s at the writing of this book, notes that Casper was unpredictable and could not be trusted. Without a moment's notice, he could turn from being a good-natured buddy, to a beast, and suddenly would "beat the hell out of you."

McQuistin, like other Baldies, spent time in the workhouse for crimes committed as a youth. While incarcerated, authorities helped him plan his future. On one occasion, which stands out in his memory, he was forced by workhouse supervisors to choose from among three girls who were sending him letters. Only one girl was allowed to write to him at a time.

"I laid the letters on the bed in front of me and thought about which ones made me feel the best, and that was the girl I chose."

This is how McQuistin selected his future wife, Maralee. She stuck with him through decades of thick and thin.

McQuistin was arrested numerous times as a young man and was not always cooperative. On one occasion, he pulled a pony of beer from an inside coat pocket and, during the booking process, smashed it over a police officer's head. The cops beat McQuistin so badly that when

Maralee and his mother came to pick him up, they didn't recognize him.

He continued to suffer from hot-headedness, which led him to commit road rage during his 60s. McQuistin, a former boxer, followed and beat up a driver half his age whom he felt was driving badly. But one beating didn't quite satisfy McQuistin. He returned to his car and followed the driver further down the road, baiting him into one more fight. This time he was arrested and hauled into court.

At the hearing, after studying details of the case, the judge looked from one man to the other as they stood before his bench, then leaned in closer and asked the hard-bodied McQuistin, "How old are you?"

He has since mellowed, atoning for his past. He turned out to be a regular guy in the end, giving up drinking and dedicating his life to his friends and family and making certain that, with every action, he is doing the next right thing.

I can vouch for McQuistin being a good guy. When I have the good fortune of running into him, he recites poetry to me, kisses me on the cheek, and calls me Darlin.' He's one bad old boy gone good.

In Closing

And so, in closing, I leave the recent past alone. No sense begging for that perfect pair of concrete overshoes to wear into the cold and muddy depths of the mighty Mississippi. I have only scratched the surface in recording the history of Minneapolis underworld, and the process leaves me with questions. I wonder, why do we tend to make the wealthy our heroes? And what kind of compromises do our politicians have to make every day? Does the spirit of the Citizens' Alliance still survive in the Minneapolis business community?

I have left many stones unturned in my humble effort to understand the underbelly of Minneapolis and I hope that others, with courage and skills far greater than mine, will go on to tell more of this fascinating story.

And yes, Virginia, there *is* a Mr. X!

"There is a heroism in crime as well as in virtue. Vice and infamy have their altars and their religion."

William Hazlitt *(1778-1830) British essayist*

Index

Alderman, Israel "Ice Pick Willie": Enforcer for the Bermans, 57
Aldrich, Cyrus Colonel: Land Speculator, 18
Alexander, Ferris, 96, 97, 99, 140, 198
Ames, Frederick W., Colonel: Superintendant Minneapolis Police, 31
Ames, Albert Alonzo (Doc): Minneapolis "Godfather of Crime", 27
Anderesch, Wesley: Witness to Liggett Murder, 148
Appelt. William, 120

Banks, Tommy: Organized Crime Member, 48, 57, 86, 121, 167
Barnett, Big Mose: Minneapolis Organized Crime Member, 60, 120, 121, 132
Benton, H. G.: Secretary of Minneapolis Real Estate Board, 57
Berman, "Chickie": Minneapolis Organized Crime Member, 57, 151, 163, 172
Berman, Davie "The Jew": Minneapolis Organized Crime Member, 151, 163, 172
Berman, Davie: Organized Crime Member, 83, 172, 173, 174, 175
Bevans, Jack: Minneapolis Organized Crime Member, 138
Birkeland, Knute B. Reverend: Murder Victim, 66
Blar, Peter: Minneapolis Theater Owner, 31
Blumenfield, Isadore: Minneapolis organized Crime Member, 57, 58, 157, 158, 159, 160, 161, 162, 163, 164, 165
Brackett, George A.: Minneapolis Mayor, 23
Bronfman, Harry: Canadian Distiller, 48
Brown, Al: Founder of the Baldies, 184
Brownstein, "Brownie": Minneapolis Organized Crime Member, 162
Bruce, Olof Ludwig: Publisher and Murderer, 66
Brunskill, Frank: Minneapolis Chief of Police, 67, 73, 120, 139
Buchanan, James: United States President, 15, 16
Burke, Jack: Twin City Boxer (Pugilist), 52
Burnquist, Joseph A. A.: Minnesota Governor, 49

Calderwood. W. G.: Secretary of the MN State Prohibition Committee, 119, 120
Capone, Al: Chicago Organized Crime Member, 9, 116, 132, 158, 173
Capper-Volstead Act, 65
Capra, Jack: Minneapolis Organized Crime Member, 125, 177, 186
Cargill, William Wallace: Minneapolis C of C Member, 61
Casper, James "Deuce": Founder of the Baldies, 181, 183
Christenson, Ruth L., 102
Citizens' Alliance, 129
Clare, "Red": Minneapolis Organized Crime Member, 138
Clark, Sam: Pubisher of Jim Jam Jems, 92
Clark, Genevieve A.: Jury Member who committed suicide., 40, 42
Clark, Hovey C.: Head of 1902 Hennepin Co. Grand Jury, 33
Cohen, Peter, 125

DeGood, Alex, 176
DeVito, Anthony: Murder Victim, 176
Donnelly, Stan D.: Attorney, 78
Drake Jr, Benjamin: Non-Partisan League, 63
Drews, Charles W.: Executive Secretary of Minneapolis Law & Order League, 57
Dry Cleaners' Case, 132
Dunne, Vince: Union Organizer, 130

Eastman, Seth: Army Major and Artist, 16
Ersin, Karl, 123
Evans Berman, Gladys: Wife of Davie "The Jew" Berman, 175

Fawcett, Annette, 94, 95, 96, 159
Fietek, Frank: Murder Victim, 167, 168, 169, 171
Fisk, James: New York Robber Baron, 22
Fitchette, "Coffee John": Minneapolis Police Officer, 31
Fletcher, Loren, 24
Forestal, Frank: Minneapolis Chief of Police, 58
. Foshay, Wilber B: Founder of Foshay Securities & Tower, 34
Foulkes, George E.: Investigator, 109, 110
Frank Azzone, John: Hit man, 177
Franklin Steele: Fort Snelling Sutler, 14, 15, 16

Goff, Art, 120
Goldman, Abe: Canadia Organized Crime Member, 48
Gordon, Gordon Lord: Racketeer, 20
Gorham Press, 123
Gottlieb, Paul: Minneapolis Organized Crime Member, 133, 139
Gould, Jay: New York Robber Baron, 22, 25, 26, 197, 200
Graham, Archibald Graham Dr.: New York Investor, 16
Greeley, Horace: Founder of Liberal Republican Party, 22, 23
Green Sheet, 123, 124, 125
Guilford, Howard: Murdered Investigative Journalist, ii, 133, 138, 142, 147, 150

Harrison, H. G.: Minneapolis C of C's First President, 61
Heiskell, William King: Land Agent, 16
Henley H. H.: Foshay Business Partner, 36
Hicks, Darby, 123
Hirschfield, Leo: Green Sheet Publisher, 123
Hodges. Mayme, 66, 68
Hoy, Michael: Minneapolis Police Officer, 24
Humphrey, Hubert H.: Minneapolis Mayor, U.S. Vice President, 83, 200

Jackson, Walter: Wheat Smuggler, 113
Jaffa, Harry: Minneapolis Organized Crime Member, 133, 139

Jankowitz, Abe: Minneapolis Organized Crime Member, 133
Jesup, Thomas S.: Quartermaster General, Fort Snelling, 15
John B. Floyd: U.S. Secretary of War, 14, 16

Kasherman, Arthur: Murdered Investigative Journalist, 84, 138, 150, 151, 152
Keegan, Owen: Minneapolis Police Officer, 24
Keffler, Jack: Slot Machine Collector, 120
Kenney, Sister Elizabeth, 87
Kline, Marvin: Minneapolis Mayor, 83, 89, 151, 173

Lathorp, Lorin A.: American Consul in Nassau, 47
Latimer, Thomas: Minneapolis Mayor, 58, 172
Liggett, Walter: Murdered Investigative Journalist, ii, 29, 57, 70, 73, 90, 133, 138, 139, 141, 142, 143, 144, 146, 150, 158, 159, 198, 199
Loomis, J.: Land Commissioner for Northern Pacific Railway, 21
Lupino. Rocky: Hit man, 134, 176, 178, 185
Lyon, Hiram A.: Minneapolis Jewel Smuggler, 110
Lyons, Evangeline: Smuggler, Poodle Girl, 112

Magnie, A.J.: Wheat Smuggler, 113
Manahan, James: Minnesota Congressman, 64
Mancino, John: Criminal, 177
Martinson, Oscar: Hennepin County Sheriff, 49, 79
Mather, **John C.**, 16, 19
Mather, Mrs. Ralph: Accident Victim, 81
McCormick, Robert R. Colonel: Publisher of the Chicago Tribune, 59
McQuistin, George: Baldy, 187
Megaarden, Philip: Hennepin County Sheriff, 31
Merriam, George N.: Minnesota Governor, 23, 25
Midwest American: Muckraking Newspaper, ii, 67, 70, 133, 141, 145, 159, 161; Published by Walter Liggett, 70
Millik, Perry: Baldie and Member of Organized Crime, 185, 186
Minneapolis Chamber of Commerce, 61, 63, 64, 65
Morgan, Ed: Minneapolis Organized Crime Member, 138
. Morrill, Rev. Giulian L, 93
Moses, Phillip: Minneapolis Organized Crime Member, 132
Murphy, Charles: American Liquor Exporter in Bahamas, 47

Nash, William M. (Bud): Hennepin County Attorney, 49
Naugle, Oliver T.: Hennepin County Grand Jury Foreman, 59
Near, J. M.: Editor of the Saturday Press, 132
Near vs. Minnesota: First Amendment Court Case, 140
Non-Partisan League: Political Third Party, 141
Nye, Mayor Wallace G.: Minneapolis Mayor, 79

O'Connor System, 45, 78, 79

Ogdahl . Tommy: Baldy, Minneapolis Alderman, 180, 187
Olshan, Mort, 124
Olson. Floyd B.: Minnesota Governor, 54, 59, 60, 67, 69, 70, 73, 95, 120, 121, 129, 130, 132, 138, 141, 143, 144, 146, 152, 160
Oppenheimer, Will: Attorney, 78, 81

Passolt, Melvin: Investigator, 68, 120, 122
Patterson, George: Minneapolis Organized Crime Member, 125, 186
Peavey , Frank Hutchinson: Minneapolis C of C Member, 61
Pettit, John U.: Indiana Congressman, 15

Rabinovitch, Harry: Canadian Organized Crime Member, 48, 51
Ramsey, Alexander: Minnesota Governor and Speculator, 25, 27, 28
Rice, Henry M., 15
Ritten , Louis N.: Minneapolis Alderman, 73, 74
Rogers, Roy: Minneapolis Businessman, 60
Ruff , Werner H.: Racketeer, 73

Safford, George B.: Head of Ant-Saloon League, 49
Scavo, Sandy Roy: Criminal, 177
Schall , Senator Thomas D., 149
Schell, Richard: New York Investor, 16
Scher , "Flippy": Minneapolis Organized Crime Member, 139
Schullo , Tony: Teamster, Racketeer, 134, 136
Shapiro , Sam, 132, 133
Siegel, Bugsy: Murder Incorporated, 81, 172, 175
Smolak the Polak, 177
Sodini, J.C.: Proprietor of the Columbia Theater, 31
Sousa, John Philip: Composer of "Fosahy Tower Washington Memorial, 37
Strong , A. W., 129
Swing City, 167, 170

The Public Press: Muckraking Newspaper, 152, 154
Tilseth ,Tut: Baldy, 186
Twin Cities Reporter: Muckraking Newspaper, 138

Von Wald , Pearl: Witness to Kasherman Murder, 152, 153

Ward . Charlie: President of Brown & Bigelow, 77, 80, 82, 160
Weisman, Michael: Minneapolis Organized Crime Member, 48, 49, 51
William Lepora, Louis: Criminal, 177
Woodward, John: Racketeer, 73

Younger, Cole: Northfield Bank Robber, 30

Bibliography

Alexandria Gazette (Alexandria, VA. "Lord Gordon; Canada; Minnesota; Mr. Clarke; Manitoba; St. Paul; Minneapolis." Juy 21, 1874: 2.

Duluth Daily News . "Flaws in the Law. A Market Authority Discusses the State Inspection Humbug ." January 5, 1889: 4.

Grand Forks Herald . "Fur Thefts Are Wide in Area Minneapolis Saloon Headquarters for Distribution of Stolen Property ." February 11, 1915: 1.

" Police Given Commands to Shoot to Kill Chief Martinson of Minneapolis Takes Course to Stop Crime." *Aberdeen American* , 12-15-16: 6.

The Appeal Newspaper.Appeal-Western Appeal. "ROMANCE OF MODERN SMUGGLING." December 31, 1898: 1.

Weekly Wisconsin Patriot . "The Minnesota Humbug ." June 30, 1855: 2.

(AP). "Odds-Maker Says He Combats Fixes; Minneapolis Man Denies He Runs a Gambling House." *New York Times*, September 8, 1961.

"Ames is Again Indicted." *The St. Paul Globe*, 2-6-1903: 3.

AP. "TEAMSTERS UNION FETES TONY SHULLO." *Daily Journal*, April 21, 1954.

Article. "Charge Hennepin County Attorney Aids Whisky Plot Horrible State of Affairs, is Court Verdict Liquor." *Duluth News-Tribune*, 05-12-1920: 1.

Article. "Charge Reed act Violated. Five Men, including Hennepin County Sheriff, Placed under Arrest." *Duluth News Tribune*, 03-24-1920: 8.

Article. "Nash Held for Winnipeg Booze Importing Deal Hennepin County Attorney Accused of Conspiracy to Import Whiskey." *Aberdeen American*, 5-12-1920: 1.

Article. "Paid Nash $1,000 in Whisky Plot, Wiseman Says Arrests Were to be Made County Cases." *Duluth News-Tribune*, 5-28-1920: 1.

Asbury, Herbert. *Sucker's Progress: An Informal History of Gambling in America*. Perseus Books Group, 2003.

Berman, Susan. *Easy Street*. Random House Publishing Group, 1983.

Birmingham, Stephen. *The Rest of Us: The Rise of America's Eastern European Jews*. Syracuse University Press, 1999.

Blum, Geoffrey. *The View from Calgary*. Prescott, AZ: The Bruce Hamilton Company, 1997.

Bryan, Dan. *The Big Con: Jay Gould, a British "Lord", and a $1 million bribe gone wrong*. n.d. http://www.americanhistoryusa.com/big-con-jay-gould-a-british-lord-million-bribe/ (accessed September 7, 2012).

Calverton, V. F. "Who Killed Walter Liggett." *The Modern Monthly*, January 1936: 390-396.

"Companies Hit by Interest Rate." *Bemidji Daily Pioneer*, 4-5-1913: 1.

"Dakota Election Causes Stir on Board of Trade." *The Day Book*, 11-13-1916: 30.

Davis, Forrest. "Liggett Killing Brings Long Political Strife to a Stirrling Climax." *World Telegram*, December 18, 1935.

El Paso Herald Home Edition SPORTS. "Southwestern Towns Book Boxing Bouts for July 4th (KID CANN)." June 30, 1915: 7.

Evening Post (New York, NY) Volume: LVI. "The Great West--The Minnesota Humbug ." May 5, 1857: 1.

Evening Times, Grand Forks. "Capture Made On Soo Train Cando Seizure Followed More Activity--Other Developments Due ." March 26, 1912: 1.

Ferris Alexander, Appellant, v. Richard Thornburgh, in His Official Capacity Only Asattorney General of the United States, Appellee.united States of America, Appellee, v. Ferris Jacob Alexander, Sr., A/k/a Pete Saba, Peter Saba,paul Saba, Jo. 943 F.2d 825 (United States Court of Appeals, Eighth Circuit., March 13, 1991).

Grand Forks Herald . "Confesses He is a Party of Smuggling Aliens into U. S." August 29, 1915: 1.

"Labor Payoffs Investigated." *Omaha World Herald*, 1954: 8.

Lambert, Richard Oulahan and William. "Scandal in the Bahamas I." *Life Magazine* , 2/3/1967 : (58) 60 - 74.

Liggett, Edith, interview by captain of Detectives A. Marxen. *Report On Shooting of Walter Liggett* (December 9, 1935).

Liggett, Edith, interview by Detective Supervisor John Hilborn. *Statement of Mrs. Walter Liggett after Liggett Shooting* (December 9, 1935).

Lorin Andrews Lathrop . n.d. http://www.knoxhistory.org/authors/lathrop.htm (accessed 11 12, 2012).

Mayer, George H. *Political Career of Floyd B Olson*. St. Paul: Minnesota Historical Society Press, 1987.

"McHugh Saved from Questions." *The Bemidji Daily Pioneer*, 2-20-1913: 1.

Millikan, William. *A Union Against Unions: The Minneapolis Citizens Alliance and Its Fight Against Organized Labor*. St. Paul: Minnesota Historical Society Press, 2003.

Minneapolis Journa. "The Poodle Girl. is Arrested in Wisconsin Charged with Smuggling ." October 29, 1900: 6.

Minneapolis Journal . "Loaded with Gems. No Wonder Ma'amselle's Poodle Finally Died of Indigestion ." October 6, 1900: 2.

Minneapolis Morning Tribune. "Big Smuggling Ring Is Unearthed Here." August 24, 1912: 15.

Minneapolis Morning Tribune. "Three Change Pleas to Guilty in Liquor Plot." November 11, 1922: 10.

Minneapolis Star. "Cann Clan Outlets Listed." October 21, 1960: 1.

Minnesotian-Herald. "The "Lord" Gordon Fiasco." July 12, 1873: 2.

Mr. Pettit, Select Committee 35th Congress House of Representatives. "Fort Snelling investigation." Washington D.C., 1858.

New York Herald. "Another Account. High-Handed Proceedings-the Noble Lord Spending Money Freely ." July 11, 1873: 7.

New York Times. "Lyon a Magnate in Grain." June 1, 1910.

O. "The New Bedford , Fort Schuyler, and Fort Snelling Land Sales - Evidence of a Grand Plumder Combination of New York Policitians." *New York Times*, April 12, 1858.

Pianin, Patrick Marx and Eric. "'Kid Cann' Outlived Many 'Persecutors,' Prefers a Quiet Life." *Minneapolis Star*, December 13, 1976: 13A.

Reichard, Gary W. "Hubert H. Humphrey." *Minnesota History*, Summer 1998: 50-67.

RICHARD O. DAVIES, RICHARD G. ABRAM. *BETTING THE LINE: SPORTS WAGERING IN AMERICAN LIFE.* Ohio State University Press, 2001.

Richards, Ray. "$100,000 Paid 'Bugsy' by Rich Friend Probed." *Los Angeles Examiner Washington Bureau*, July 19, 1947.

Schuldberg, Meyer, interview by Detectives Kramer & Eisenkramer. *Statement of Meyer Schuldberg Following Liggett Killing* (December 9, 1935).

Sifakis, Carl. *The Mafia Encyclopedia.* Infobase Publishing, 2005.

Spinelli, Lawrence. *Dry Diplomacy: The United States, Great Britain, and Prohibition.* Rowman & Littlefield, 2007.

Springfield Republican (Springfield, MA) Issue: 51. "The Mysterious Lord Gordon Who Outwitted Jay Gould. A Remarkable Yarn About an Aristocratic Impostor ." September 3, 1905: 15.

St. Paul Globe. "His Finish as a Reformer (DOC AMES)." April 16, 1901: 4.

St. Paul Pioneer Pressq. "Obscene Mail Charge Names Mrs. Fawcett." July 9, 1938: 1.

Staff. "If There's a Pie Anywhere, Foshay's Finger Is in It!" *Seattle Daily Times*, March 22, 1929: 24.

The Bemidji Daily Pioneer. "Companies Hit By Interest Rate; Farmer Elevator Concerns Must Pay Seven Percent for Five and One Half Money Say Probers." April 5, 1913: 1.

The Bemidji Daily Pioneer. "Martinson Gets Two Years In Leavenworth." July 31, 1920: 1.

The Day Book. "Dakota Election Causes Stir on Board of Trade." November 13, 1913: 30.

The Minneapolis Journal. "Chamber of Commerce Edition." March 30, 1903: 1.

"The Right to Bargain." *Springfield Union*, 1954: 11.

The Rothschilds' Story. 2011.
    http://www.sudburylivingmagazine.ca/content/heritage/Rothschild06132011.aspx (accessed September 7, 2012).

Thomis, Wayne. "Murder in Minneapolis." *Chicago Sunday Tribune*, Feburary 9, 1936: 7.

Time Magazine. "CORPORATIONS: Big House to Big Board." July 5, 1948.

United States of America, Appellee, v. Steve Thomas, Appellant.united States of America, Appellee, v. Frank Schullo and Anthony Petrangelo, Appellants. 508 F.2d 1200 (United States Court of Appeals, Eighth Circuit, February 12, 1974).

"Unknown." *Springfield Republican*, 5-19-1903.

"Weisman Related Whisky Conspiracy." 14 1921, January.

Wingard, Earl. "Kid Cann Says: I've Sold Out and Am Leaving Town." *Minneapolis Tribune*, January 27, 1952.

Wire, AP:. "Twin City Raids Hit Gamblers." *Aberdeen Daily News*, 6-22-1971: 1.

Writer, Staff. "These Men Hate the "Right to Work" Law." *Times-Picayune*, 6-27-1954: 22.

—. "PHILANTHROPY: A Case of Self-Help." *Time Magazine*, July 11, 1960.

ABOUT THE AUTHOR

Elizabeth Johanneck is author of *Hidden History of the Minnesota River Valley*, and *Twin Cities Prohibition; Minnesota's Blind Pigs and Bootleggers*, published by The History Press. She grew up on a farm near Wabasso in southwestern Minnesota with seven brothers and a sister. She graduated with a B.S. degree in business administration from Southwest State University in Marshall, Minnesota. She currently resides in Richfield, Minnesota